Unveiling Your Hidden Power

Other Books in This Series

Coming Into Freedom:
H. Emily Cady's Lessons in Truth for the 21st Century

Identifying with the Infinite:
Lillian DeWaters' Science of Ascension for the 21st Century

Experiencing the Miracle:
The Essence of the Course in Miracles for the 21st Century

Each of these volumes is Ruth L. Miller's modern-language version of the original text. She has removed gender bias, used shorter sentences and paragraphs, cited sacred sources from multiple spiritual traditions, and has added summary points, headings, and exercises for each section.

An Overview of Their Teachings

Healing by Words Alone
Understanding America's New Thought Healers & Teachers

Unveiling Your Hidden Power

EMMA CURTIS HOPKINS'
METAPHYSICS FOR
THE 21ST CENTURY

modern interpretation by
Ruth L. Miller

2nd edition

SPIRIT BOOKS

www.portalcenterpress.com

Unveiling Your Hidden Power: Emma Curtis Hopkins'
Metaphysics for the 21st Century

1st edition © 2007 Ruth L. Miller
published by WiseWoman Press
ISBN: 978-0-945385-05-9

2nd edition © 2024 Ruth L. Miller
Published by **SPIRIT BOOKS,**
an imprint of Portal Center Press
www.portalcenterpress.com

ISBN: 978-1-936902-51-4

Printed in the U.S.A.

Acknowledgments for the 1st Edition

This work would not have been possible without the support of all my friends, colleagues, students, and family. I particularly want to thank Sandra Tabb for accepting this title as the first offered by WiseWoman Press, Ayama and Con for their ongoing support, patience and understanding over the years of discovering, writing, and teaching this material, Nelson Maxwell for insisting that it "had to be done," all the students who have read and listened to and worked with it, and the Terranovas for getting the Emma material out to the world.

Thanks also go to Robert Winterhalter of the Society for the Study of Metaphysical Religions, for seeing the value of making this work available, and to Sandra and Barbara at WiseWoman Press for bringing it, finally, into print.

Special appreciation goes to Rev. Jody Stevenson, who introduced me and the rest of my ministry class to Emma's role and works, and to Rev. Vici Derrick, whose love for Emma's writings inspired me to take a closer look.

Finally, to all the students who have worked through various drafts of this material over the years, your enthusiasm for the material and your questions about the way it was presented are the reason this book came to be. Many, many thanks to all!

Acknowledgements for the 2nd Edition

It's been 2 decades since I first typed the words on these pages, and so many things have happened since! Yet, through it all, month in and month out, classes have gathered to study Emma's profound teachings, using this book, or the Workbook that's based on it. Wow! Many thanks to Michael and Charlene Terranova for making the first edition of this work available to so many for so long!

All those students and all those teachers have found the power in themselves because they took the time and effort to read these pages and do the practices that Beloved Emma laid out for us. That is amazing to me, and I am deeply honored to have been a part of their awakening – and grateful that they did so.

For this edition, and the feedback that led to the changes that are in it, I am deeply grateful to the students who have worked with me through the years. All of you have contributed to my understanding and helped me discover new depths of our hidden power, as well.

--*rlm*

Contents

PREFACE	VII
A New Science	viii
A Second Generation of Scientists	xi
An Expanded Interpretation of the Science	xiv
This Book	xiv
PART ONE: THE TWELVE LESSONS	1
LESSON ONE: RETURNING TO OUR TRUE NATURE	3
Naming Our Good	5
Experiencing Our Good	7
A Higher Vision	9
A Name of Power	12
A New Discipline	16
Practice	18
Monday mornings: Focus on Being	18
Daily:	20
The Metaphors	20
The Number: ONE	20
The Precious Stone: Jasper, the White Stone.	20
The Apostle, or Power of the Soul: Judas, the Intellect.	21
LESSON TWO: REMISSION—NEGATING THE UNREAL	23
Negating Belief in Absence	25
Negating the Limitations of Matter	27
Negating Belief in Evil	30
Experiencing Freedom	31
Negating Distress and Pain	33
Cleansing the Soul	35
Beyond the Five—Our Personal Negations	38
The Practice	41
Tuesday mornings:	41
Daily:	42
The Metaphors	42
The Number: TWO	42
The Stone: Sapphire, wisdom & peace	43
The Apostle: Simon, Zeal	43
LESSON THREE: FORGIVENESS—AFFIRMATIONS	45
Negations as Openings for Affirmations	47

The Power of Affirming	49
General Affirmations	52
Personal Affirmations	58
The Practice.	59
Wednesday Mornings:	59
Daily:	60
The Metaphors	60
The Number: THREE	60
The Stone: Chalcedony	61
The Apostle: Judas Thaddeus, Fearlessness & Freedom	61
LESSON FOUR: FAITH—THE FOUNDATION	**63**
Confidence to Command	66
The Key	68
No Condition too Great	69
Generating Faith	71
Demonstrations & Experience	Error! Bookmark not defined.
A New Covenant	77
The Power Is Within	79
Faith Made Manifest	80
The Practice	82
Thursday mornings:	82
Daily:	84
The Metaphors	85
The Number: FOUR	85
The Stone: Emerald	85
The Apostle: James, Confidence in Discernment	85
LESSON FIVE: WORKS—THE WORD OF FAITH	**87**
The Power of Our Thoughts	89
Words of Faith	90
Freedom	91
Uncovering the Real World	92
Opening to the Power	94
Transforming the Body	96
The Practice	98
Friday mornings:	98
Daily:	98
The Metaphors	98
The Number: FIVE	98
The Stone: Sardonyx	99

The Apostle: Thomas, a Fool for the Christ 99
LESSON SIX. UNDERSTANDING THE SECRET 101
The Power Revealed   102
What's happening, here?   103
Acknowledging the Gift   104
The Soul's Science   106
Focus & Discernment   109
I AM   110
The Practice   112
    Saturday mornings: 112
The Metaphors   112
    The Number: SIX 112
    The Stone: Sardius 112
    The Apostle: Matthew—Clear Sight, the "Gift of the Lord" 113
LESSON SEVEN: INHERITANCE—WELLSPRING OF LIFE 115
The Power of Praise   117
The Healing Ministry   120
Overcoming Fear   122
Guidelines for Treatment   124
All Methods the Same   127
The Practice.   131
    Monday Afternoons: 131
    With a Client: 131
    Daily: 133
The Metaphors.   133
    The Number: SEVEN. 133
    The Stone: Chrysolite. 134
    The Apostle: Bartholomew, Imagination. 134
LESSON EIGHT: TRUTH—RENDING THE VEIL 137
Lights in the Firmament   139
Signs of the Spirit   143
Forms Are Nothing; Light is all.   144
Guidelines for Treatment   145
The Practice.   147
    Tuesday Afternoons: 147
    With a Returning Case: 148
    Daily: 149
The Metaphors.   149
    The Number: EIGHT 149
    The Stone: Beryl 149

The Apostle: Philip, Love. 150
LESSON NINE: HOLINESS—RIGHT DISCERNMENT 151
No Accusation   152
The Joy-filled Life   154
Recognition & Acknowledgment   156
Effortlessness   157
Guidelines for Treatment   159
The Practice   160
   With a Returning Case: 160
   Daily: 161
The Metaphors   161
   The Number: NINE 161
   The Stone: Topaz 162
   The Apostle: Andrew, Strength. 162
LESSON TEN: EFFECTIVENESS—FREEDOM 165
Shaping the World   166
Permanent Healing   168
Our Perfect Gift   170
Choosing Faith Over Doubt or Fear   171
Time   176
Experiencing Joy and Peace   177
Guidelines for Treatment   180
The Practice   181
   Thursday Afternooons: 181
The Metaphors   183
   The Number: TEN 183
   The Stone: Chrysoprasus, ... 184
   The Apostle: John, God's Grace. 184
LESSON ELEVEN: THE WAY OF WISDOM 187
Will & Meekness   188
Demonstration & Redemption   191
Perfect Judgment   193
Inspiration: Empowering the Mind   195
Guidelines for Treatment   197
The Practice.   199
   Friday Afternoons: 199
   With a Returning Client: 199
   Periodically: 200
The Metaphors.   201
   The Number: ELEVEN. 201
   The Stone: Jacinth or Red Rubellite. 201

The Apostle: James, Son of Zebedee, Judgment.........201
LESSON TWELVE: LOVE—THE CROWN OF GLORY.........203
Signs & Symbols 204
Praise and Gratitude Undo Complaints 206
Transcendence 208
Guidelines for Treatment 210
Claiming Our Birthright 211
The Practice 215
   Saturday Afternoons:..215
   With a Returning client: 215
   Sunday:..216
The Metaphors 217
   The Number: TWELVE 217
   The Stone: Amethyst 217
   The Apostle: Simon Peter 218
PART TWO: COMMENTARIES... 219
THE HISTORICAL CONTEXT... 221
Emma's Experience 243
Discovered Texts 222
Modern Science 224
THE PRINCIPLES IN THE LANGUAGE OF SCIENCE 227
PART THREE..229
THE RADIANT I AM 231
ABOUT THE AUTHORS 243
BOOKS BY EMMA CURTIS HOPKINS 241
BOOKS BY RUTH L. MILLER 251
COMMENTS FROM READERS 254

Preface

Amazing things were happening in American religious communities between 1845 and 1925: remarkable new ways of thinking were introduced and new roles and forms of the Christian church were tried. Among other things, during those years, women began to take leadership roles, and, where their ideas were not accepted by existing authorities, they built their own schools of theology and divinity, training a new generation of ministers and building a whole new kind of church.

In these new churches, for the first time in nearly two thousand years of Christianity, holistic, integrative approaches were being given voice. In these churches, for the first time since the Reformation, the Gospel teachings of Jesus were given greater importance than the directives and interpretations of Paul's pastoral letters, and the many miracles of the New Testament were emphasized over the demonstrated anger of the Jehovah of the Old Testament. More, in these churches, the "feminine" aspects of religion — healing, nurturing, and supporting — were given greater importance than the traditional "masculine" focus on obedience to a higher power and authority.

The essential message offered by these new Christian churches was simple: Jesus called us to live as he did and he promised that we would do what he did "and greater."

The leaders of these new churches included Aimee Semple McPherson, Ellen White, Mary Baker Eddy, the Brooks sisters, the Rix sisters, and Myrtle and Charles

Fillmore. They formed the unabashedly American churches known as Assemblies of God, Foursquare, Christian Science, Divine Science, Unity, and Church of Truth. Pentecostal in their focus, these churches are, still today, some of the fastest growing in the world.

A NEW SCIENCE

Probably the most well-known of these new churches was launched in Massachusetts, based on the writings and teachings of Mary Baker Glover Patterson Eddy. Her Massachusetts Metaphysical College became the Church of Christ, Scientist, in Boston: "the mother church" for an international movement, and a model for many more to come.

Mrs. Eddy's success was based on several factors: her absolute conviction of the correctness of her understanding; her unrelenting commitment to sharing that understanding with as many people as possible; her effectiveness as a healer; and her experience in public relations. Her various biographies reveal a woman whose early education was based primarily on the Bible, who was widowed at an early age, and who, upon becoming involved in the first stages of the women's movement, trained for a career in homeopathy, a gentle form of healing that appealed to women of the period as an alternative to the "butchery" of traditional medicine practiced at that time.

Mary Baker Glover married an itinerant dentist, Dr. Patterson, and traveled around New England with him for some years, distributing pamphlets, writing newspaper releases, and delivering lectures as a way to attract patients.

In the early 1860s, according to many documents, Mary Patterson was healed of life-long pain through the efforts of a "mental healer" from Maine: Phineas Parkhurst Quimby. Quimby believed that all human ailments were the product of wrong beliefs, taught by ministers and doctors, and he used the Bible and the force of his own personality to help people shift those beliefs. Mary Baker Patterson, being one of his successes, became one of his most public advocates over the next few years. In 1866, however, Mary took a fall. When she returned to Quimby to relieve her of these new pains, however, she found that he hadn't taken care of his own well-being and had died, leaving her on her own.

Having been relieved of her symptoms once before, Mrs. Patterson knew it was possible. Having seen that the key to that healing was in her understanding of the Bible, she moved into a boarding house, where she focused all her attention on internalizing the healing doctrine of Jesus. And, after a few weeks, the symptoms were gone.

Over the next few months of practicing her new understanding, she took her journal notes and transformed them into a pamphlet for her patients. And, as she moved around New England with her husband, teaching her new approach and healing patients with her words, she became well-known throughout the region; local newspapers happily recorded her successes.

Then, in 1875, Mary settled in Lynne, Massachusetts, divorced Doctor Patterson, published her classic, Science and Health with Key to the Scriptures, and established a little school to train healing practitioners. One of her students, Asa Eddy, proposed to her that they marry and move the school into Boston, where it could expand. They did both that next year, and by 1884 they were operating an adult-school with dormitories and offices, an association of graduates, and a regular publication, The *Christian Science Journal*.

The combination of her skills and commitment with his resources was powerful, indeed, and their work flourished. Dozens of practitioners were trained each year and went out into the world with their new skills and copies of her book, *Science and Health with Keys to the Scriptures*, sustained in their beliefs by Mrs. Eddy and the testimonies of other students through the *Journal*. It wasn't long before their church was established, along with an internal publishing house and a "good news" newspaper, *The Christian Science Monitor*. Before the end of the century, the school was dissolved into the church and the institution known as the Christian Science Church was well-established in the American landscape, with a world-renowned newspaper.

The church remained almost exactly as Mrs. Eddy had intended throughout the 20th century, following guidelines she had written in 1893. The church-run newspaper, *The Christian Science Monitor*, remains one of the most respected periodicals in the world. The church's practices have received some "bad press," however, as modern medical techniques have improved to the point where refusal of medical assistance for a sick or injured child seems more like abuse than religious zeal. Nonetheless, at the end of the century, virtually every city in America boasted several Churches of Christ, Scientist and at least one Christian Science Reading Room. In the 21st century, however, these churches are being dissolved, and the Reading Rooms with them.

A SECOND GENERATION OF SCIENTISTS

Mrs. Eddy was determined that her students succeed, and so insisted that they followed her instructions to the "T". Sadly, though, as often happens, this codification of principles and processes into one way of thinking and acting left out a significant range of possibilities — and people. As early as 1884, there were tensions among the senior students and practitioners of Mary Eddy's enterprise, and some broke away to form their own groups, based on different interpretations and expectations.

Without a doubt, the most influential of these was Emma Curtis Hopkins. Born Josephine Emma Curtis, she was also a New Englander, raised on a family farm in Connecticut, the eldest of a large family whose father served, and was severely maimed, in the Civil War. In her late teens, Emma trained to become a teacher, married George Hopkins soon after, and had a son. They were living in New Hampshire in 1883, when a neighbor invited her to attend an informal gathering with Mary Baker Eddy.

Well-versed in the classics and philosophy, as well as the sciences of her day, Emma was skeptical of Mrs. Eddy's ideas as presented that afternoon, but she had the opportunity to try them out soon after, when she and her husband became ill. To her amazement, her neighbor's procedures worked. So, leaving her son at home with her younger sister and husband, Emma went to Boston and completed the six-week basic practitioner's course with Mrs. Eddy in December of 1883, exchanging tuition for editing work on the Journal.

In October of 1885, however, after months of commuting between her home and Boston, often staying in Boston for weeks at a time, Emma was discharged without explanation. Letters between the devoted disciple and her teacher suggest that Emma's references to "other mystical writers" in her editorials, even though flattering to Mrs. Eddy, was unacceptable; there was one teacher in the Christian Science church and no others were to be deemed worthy of mention.

Emma lost little time. Invited to be interim editor of J.A. Swarts' Mind Cure journal, she and her family moved to Chicago that winter and opened the Emma Curtis Hopkins Theological Seminary with Mary Plunkett in February. Following her teacher's lead, she made good use of the media: besides serving as interim editor of a magazine, she advertised in the local paper for her classes and healing sessions, wrote regular articles, gave regular public lectures, and established the Hopkins Association of graduates, with its own newsletter and chapters.

Like Mrs. Eddy, she encouraged her graduates to go out into the world and take their new understandings to new communities. And, like her teacher, she taught thousands and was prevailed upon by her students to form a church and ordain ministers.

Unlike her teacher, though, Emma refrained from insisting that only her words and her understanding should be followed. She encouraged her students to find their own words and form their own practice — or schools — in whatever way they were called by the

Infinite Presence upon which she encouraged them to rely. She also associated herself and her work with the women's movement, as demonstrated by the placement of her booth in the Women's Pavilion rather than attempting to join the Parliament of Religions at the Chicago World's Fair.

More than that, Emma refused to create an institution. Once the movement was well launched and others had formed schools and churches of their own, she closed up shop. She dissolved her seminary, sold her belongings, and began an itinerant life. Every few months, for the next thirty years, she moved from one hotel or guest room to another, based primarily on the East Coast but traveling to Europe, the Midwest, New Mexico, and San Francisco when invited.

As a result of all the classes and trainings she offered, Emma Hopkins became known as "the teacher of teachers" and her students were the founders of numerous schools and churches, the best-known being Unity, Divine Science, and Religious Science (now Centers for Spiritual Living), touching the lives of millions, around the world.

In 1924, following a series of heart failures which she described in one of her letters as, "not so much an illness, but rather God terminating a career,"[1] Emma taught her last student, Ernest Holmes, who went on to write *Science of Mind* and to found the Religious Science Institute in Los Angeles, California. The following spring, we're told, in her bedroom on the family farm, as she listened to one of her students read a favorite passage of the Bible, Emma's spirit left her body.

---

[1] This is from a series of letters quoted extensively in Gail Harley's *Emma Curtis Hopkins, Forgotten Founder of New Thought*.

AN EXPANDED INTERPRETATION OF THE SCIENCE

Emma Hopkins expanded significantly on the work of Mary Baker Eddy, incorporating into it her own understandings of the great teachings of Eastern and Western philosophy. She provided clarity and intellectual substance to a movement that had been based on acceptance of authority, and she developed a bridge from the mystical and metaphysical writings of past ages to the reader's current experience.

Emma's message was that Jesus the Nazarene was a master teacher showing humanity how to experience unity with the divine. She taught that he had a 12-point doctrine which, if understood fully and practiced regularly, would enable the practitioner to accomplish many of the same works that he and his disciples had demonstrated, as well as whatever other works were specific to the student's situation. Her lessons were designed to help the student overcome 2000 years of conditioning to weakness by the organized church, in order to experience the power in the higher Truth of Jesus' teachings.

THIS BOOK

This volume "translates" Emma Hopkins' 12 lessons presented 1885-1918, from her rhetorical Victorian English to modern American prose. Along with various handouts and pamphlets, the three primary texts used are: *High Mysticism, Scientific Christian Mental Practice*, and *Resumé*. Every attempt has been made to be true to the essence of the teachings while clarifying the teacher's intention and limiting or explaining her many references to people and texts — which, while familiar to her 19th Century audiences, are often strange and even daunting to the 21st Century reader.

Emma's first six lessons focus on establishing the individual's own health and well-being, while lessons 7-12 expand on the same principles, applying them to work with others, which Emma called our ministry.

At the end of each lesson, her references to crystals (or "stones"), the "soul-powers" of the Apostles, and numbers are explained. Each chapter also describes her recommended practice.

Her general guidelines for living in accordance with our highest selves are as follows:

1. Be cheerful under all circumstances; to be cheerful is to be praise-full.
2. Sit down at a certain time every day and write down on paper what your idea of Good is. Write the highest ideas of Good you have... such a practice will pin you down to the truth and it is in Truth that there is power
3. Take two of the 12 doctrines (lessons) and repeat them each day. Spend an hour in the morning reasoning out the lessons that address your own nature (chapters 1-6) and an hour in the afternoon on lessons addressing the people around you and your environment (your ministry — chapters 7-12).
4. By going over and over the lessons we come nearer the healing feeling. Use this book as a starting point for your focused time; meditate on the material and your experiences; act accordingly.

She tells us that, as we take the twelve doctrines of this metaphysical Science and reason out two of them each day, "the Truth of them makes you like a harp in the fingers of Love, so enchanting will be your silent mind to the world-hurt traveler and so blessed will your voice sound to the child bruised by human hardships." More and more people, she says, will find their maladies falling away in your presence, simply because you have become firmly established in Truth.

May you find this book a useful introduction to the remarkable teachings of a powerful healer — and may you know, with the thousands of students who have gone before you, the joy and well-being of a life based in her Science of Metaphysics.

--rlm

PART ONE:

The Twelve Lessons

PREFACE

The lessons in this Science are lessons in consciousness, your pure Intelligence. There are twelve aspects of consciousness, represented by the twelve Apostles of the early Christian church, and you must be awake in every one of them. The twelve lessons herein teach us to realize them all, leaving nothing undone.

There are twelve conditions of human life that may be met with twelve truths, to be found in all religions, around the world. These twelve conditions are represented by the twelve Apostles and, when they have been met by Truth, you may be sure that your life will be free, glad, and powerful.

Mind is composed of twelve powers. When your mind exercises these twelve powers, the twelve aspects of consciousness shine like polished jewels. They make a perfect foundation for an absolute demonstration of the Spirit within each of us, and so are described in the biblical Revelation as "foundation stones."

The first six lessons in this work describe the beautiful powers of your mind as to your own experience and judgment. The last six relate to your surroundings.

Let the mind go step by step: one lesson seems to be all, then the next takes you to another level of realization, then the next—till the twelve gates of understanding are opened.

The first time you go the rounds of these twelve lessons, you may not show much difference in character or power, but be patient: the second time, the third time, the hundredth time around these statements, and how shining your life and mind become!

Lesson One: Returning To Our True Nature

The first lesson gives us the foundation idea, the truth of our nature. It is the Statement of Being: that which IS. It may be found in almost the same words through all the sacred books of the world. It's the footpath, the way by which all miracles have been performed.

We start on the path by finding out what your mind is seeking and naming it. Can you name now just exactly what your mind is seeking? If you could name what you want, you'd soon be on the right track to finding it!

If I heard the unspoken sentence lying like a hidden jewel beneath your thoughts about the things you don't like or don't have, I would hear, "Good exists somewhere for me and I could be experiencing it now!" It's a universal conviction. What the whole world is seeking, the foundation thought of all beings — even in the minds of the insects — is the Good that is theirs.

Everything moves and waits for its Good. The prince reels, drunk, from the banquet hall, seeking the Good he believes he could be experiencing. The thief works in the dark, running from the daylight, seeking the Good he thinks he could be experiencing. The liquor and jewels are poor substitutes, but they're all these people know of Good.

Why do you move your right hand? You move it to get your Good. Why do you breathe? You breathe to get your Good. Why do the stones lie still and wait? They're waiting for their Good — whatever they call it.

So you see that the Good draws everything. All that you are, all that you do and say, is determined by the Good you seek. And, since the Good that you and I aim for governs everything we do and become, the Good we are seeking must be our creator, or God.[2]

Moses said that in the beginning God created all that is, "and it was good."[3] He could say this because, as it pushes and pulls us, the Good that we seek is the intelligence, the precise combination of ideas, that brings us forth. In short, the Good you are seeking created you.

The statement, "I am seeking my Good, and my Good is my God," is a simple truth. It's so simple that the tiniest child can say, "I am seeking my Good, and Good is my God because it draws and pushes and moves me on."

We are, each one of us, the center of our own universe, which extends out infinitely in all directions from where we stand. We are the unit around which our own Good swings, and if we are fully centered in our relation to our Good, and we can explain how we secured our Good, then we can begin to teach the world how to attain its Good!

Why do we say, "My Good is my God?" Can we not see that every move we make is to get some experience of what we call good to ourselves? Whatever draws you toward it, making you think it can satisfy you, governs you, and becomes your God.

---

[2] The English word, "God," comes from a German word that means "high Good."

[3] Here is the link between Emma's first lesson and the first verse of the first book of the Bible, Genesis, traditionally said to be written by Moses: "In the beginning God created heaven and earth… and it was good."

This means that Good is the governor of your life.[4] Thus it is your God!

As we acknowledge that the Good we are seeking must be our God—because it pulls and pushes us all the time to see if we can't get closer to it—we must[5] find ourselves better and better satisfied. We must experience more and more of that which we call Good. Nothing can resist the very first proclamation of Truth if we let it be spoken through us, so it's an omnipotent idea.

It's an idea found in everything, everywhere, so you speak an omnipresent idea when you say: "I seek my Good; my Good is my God. My Good is my free life. My Good is my unlimited health. My Good is my strength; my unlimited supply."

Our life, our nature, is brought forth by and seeks only the Good. You can see, then, that our Good, which is God, is everywhere present, omnipresent; it is all the power and all-powerful in our world, omnipotent; and it is wise beyond wisdom, omniscient. This is Truth. Therefore, you may take for your first idea, one word: "Good." This is the Statement of Being.

NAMING OUR GOOD

Do you hide the idea of your Good in the recesses of your mind, never expressing it? Can you see how much light might break over you and brighten your life if you would let your perfect idea of Good come up from that hidden place in your mind?

---

[4] This idea is very similar to that presented by Maxwell Maltz in the 1960s best-seller, *Psychocybernetics* (note that the Latin word *governor* comes from the Greek word, *cybernetes*.

[5] Emma's word "must" is best understood as "can't not" – we can't not experience more Good.

Our Good has many names. We can call it a perfect job or relationship, or we can go to a higher level and call it Love, Life, Truth, Substance, and Intelligence. These are also some of the names of God.

It's helpful to say that our Good is unbounded, unlimited Love. All things instinctively seek for love. Love is the highest name of God. Love is the fulfilling of the law. Love is not something that comes to us in any one man, woman, or child, and then goes away—that's only the sign of Love. The Love that is God is eternal, infinite. At the height of our spiritual teachings we find God covering us with love. We find ourselves loving all things and all people. Love is another name for life. I don't suppose it would be possible to name the Good by the magic word Love too often.

We call our Good, Truth. This will cause us to speak Truth. The Roman governor, Pilate, asked Jesus, "What is Truth?" The earliest Egyptians said, "Truth is God." Metaphysicians, repeating the idea that "Truth is God," finally came to see that it is so because telling the exact Truth about Good is an irresistible energy for bringing Good to pass. The honest statement that "My Good is my God" has all the power of Omnipotent Truth.

Metaphysicians of all cultures, tracing the cause of evil[6] conditions, have agreed that fear of evil is the only evil. But fear leaves us as we tell the Truth. By telling the Truth that our Good is our all-powerful defense and protection, dissolving all possibilities that appear

---

[6] In the 19th century, the "evil" had a broader usage than today, referring to all conditions that were less than ideal: illness, an ill-timed storm, hurtful gossip—all were, in that time, called "evils." In this work, she's referring to anything that you think of as "not good.".

unlike the Love and Life that our Good is, we can see that in every place where we proclaim divine defense, there is no evil—only the Good we are seeking. All the evil that men fear is in three words—sin, sickness, death—and the spoken Truth sets the speaker absolutely free from them.

It's not Truth to say that anyone depends upon any kind of work for their support; our work isn't the Good we are seeking. God doesn't work in the lie that someone tells when they say they're seeking a job, God works in Truth. We must tell the Truth and God will work for us. So name your Good as your unfailing supply of resources—for isn't that what you truly seek? After practicing feeling that God is your support, your old job or business will no longer be interesting. It will leave you, but you'll still have your living—you'll have wonderful miracles of support!

You can name God, your Good, as free, unlimited health. No material process can bring health, but by a metaphysical process, health will quicken and thrill all humanity.[7] The moment you feel this truth, and speak it, you catch a new breath of health, and your neighbor catches a new breath of health, as well. Everything rises to acknowledge Truth.

EXPERIENCING OUR GOOD

How shall we arrive at our Good? How shall we get hold of our Good? Not by working with our hands, for countless ages of such labor have failed.

---

[7] As more people practice the principles that Emma taught in Unity, Centers for Spiritual Awareness, Divine Science, and other spiritual organizations, or through science-based processes like Joe Dispenza's workshops, this fact is becoming "mainstream" in the culture.

But Mind speaking Truth through the lips, or thinking Truth consciously, can bring all the satisfaction that the world is seeking, for when you speak for yourself, you speak for the world.

There will be no opposition to Truth when you speak it. When you look at a drunk or miser and say he is seeking his Good, his heart will be better satisfied the instant you speak out what his unspoken instinct is feeling. He doesn't say it, himself; if he did, his life would be much more satisfying. Sometimes when you say to the sick person, mentally, that the Good he is seeking is God, and God is free health, he will get well in five minutes. His mind was unconsciously groping around for the Divine Word that could heal him, and you spoke Truth for him.

It's better if we speak our own words, but if somebody opens the door for us, it will teach us to open the door ourselves. If we don't speak our words ourselves and so are not satisfied with Good, another may speak for us, and our satisfaction will come.[8]

This Truth method brings the fulfillment of all our expectations. Be definite when you give this statement of Good, which is the Statement of Being. Speaking out continuously what we have felt and thought intuitively is the first movement toward demonstration,

---

[8] Mary Manin Morrissey described this process in her book, *Build Your Field of Dreams*, when she tells of a woman coming to her hospital bed the night before a major kidney operation and asking her, "Do you believe God can heal your kidneys?" to which Mary replied "not really," so the woman said, "Do you believe He can heal one of them?" and Mary said it seemed more possible—at which point the woman said "Then can you believe in my belief?" Mary's affirmative reply satisfied the woman and the next morning the doctors were surprised to find that Mary's kidney was completely well.

toward manifestation, toward satisfaction. No material thing can strengthen people, but the Omnipotent Truth can strengthen them all with the power of Truth.

To expect Good and to be very definite in the mind that it IS coming, is to see it coming. Expect to see it work quickly. Truth is not slow, Truth is quick. With Truth, all is NOW, for Truth does not have to make things new for you. In Truth it was so from the beginning, as the first verse of Moses reads. All Truth is waiting for you to feel and say plainly what is your Good.

A HIGHER VISION

We all have the very subtle capacity to always, at any time, look toward the Good, the Source of our being. We do so with an inner vision rather than our physical eyes. This subtle sense, this spiritual eye, is the one faculty of our soul that we're always using.

It's up to you to choose whether to make your God either the highest principle that you can comprehend or the incidents and happenings of your everyday life. There's an uplifting strength in acknowledging that my Good is Life and my Good is Truth that doesn't come to the person who says their Good, which is their God, is their car or beer or games, or any other material good.[9] What have you sought after? That was your acknowledged Good. It has marked your face and form. *The face and form always show what the thoughts proclaim as Good.*

---

[9] This tendency to name a material object, rather than unfailing Spirit, as our good is common in western culture, and is really placing an idol before God—hence the Biblical instruction: "place no other gods before me."

The mystics of all ages have learned that, when focusing their inward eye on the world around them, or their own emotions, they can manifest no beauty in their action nor effectiveness in their language. Yet, when directing their inner vision toward the un-nameable and indescribable Deity, they've astonished their own age and all ages by their miraculous performances and noble sayings.

In the *Tao Te Ching*, (written about 600 B.C.E.) we read:[10]

> Make use of the light, returning again to its Source;
>
> Your body shall be free from calamity's course,
>
> And you shall move with the Eternal at length.

"What you see is what you become" says the ancient proverb: the life that we live comes from wherever we've focused this visioning power. The mind isn't capable of bringing anything to pass, except through the inward visioning, or imagining. Indeed, it's been found that what we envision steadily causes our thinking. Then, since speech follows the direction of vision and thought, people's words soon expose why they are unfortunate or triumphant, great or inconsequent.

We collect sadness and depression from directing this mystic eye toward human faces — which is why the biblical king Solomon wept so loudly and why the prophet, Jeremiah, was brought to sickness and martyrdom as he lamented the afflictions of his people. All the symptoms or conditions that our body exhibits are

---

[10] The author of the *Tao te Ching*, or *Book of the Tao*, is usually cited as Lao Tsu, a name which translates from the Chinese as, "Ancient Master."

the accumulation of what our inner vision has seen. Sanity and soundness characterize those who do not project their inner vision toward objects that gratify the five outer senses. For, as the proverb says, it's what we see most with our inner eye, and not what we think most, that makes up our presence, power and history.

Those who look toward Heaven are invulnerable to honor or contempt, praise or disappointment. This is why all the sacred books of the world repeat one essential message: focusing attention on the Highest Good is the way of salvation from sin, sickness, misfortune, and death.

Those who focus on the qualities of the One inhabiting Eternity are ransomed from sin, disorder, and death. With the immortal and ever-young mystical eye, even those who have become aged, senile, and decrepit behold heaven—and then they leave their bodies, dropping their robes of clay, to be identified with this joy-giving vision. Had their inner eye been lifted to such heights in earlier days, they would have transfigured and renewed their flesh, instead of degrading it into death.

In the past, ignorant seekers longed so much to have this immortal faculty work good for them that they tortured their bodies and deprived themselves to set it free. But the inner vision asks no such sufferings on the part of mind or body. Left to itself it flies away to its rightful resting place. It asks only our will that it go homeward.

Whoever simply glances upward toward the Perfect Deity begins to be lifted upward into this heavenly kingdom, even as the young oak tree, straining toward the sun, lifts itself out of the rotting pulp in which it was sprouted. Lifting the inner eye to the state of Being above reason lights the two outer eyes to see the world in a new way, gives the tongue new descriptions of the world, and sets the pen to turning immortal phrases. In high moments of recognition of the light that transcends reason, men and women transcend themselves, and write more wisely than they know. Plato wrote, "No man when in his wits attains prophetic truth and inspiration, but when he receives the inspired word, his intelligence is enthralled."

This deathless ability of vision is our only power to achieve. It depends neither on thought of mind nor actions of the body. The healing of the mind to think all-powerful truth waits upon that light which only the uplifted inner, mystic eye can bring. Matter's transformation waits for the mystic eye's flawless ecstasy. Order and beauty hide their sublime mysteries until, on the Tao's magic path, our tireless inner vision speeds toward the Origin of beauty and order.

This is the arcane way of all times and cultures — a high mysticism — which, if knowingly practiced, is a science, and if unwittingly and spontaneously exercised, is called inspiration. When practiced as science (the knowledge of invariably orderly processes), inspiration follows speedily. When practiced as inspiration (occasional glimpses of greatness), great works are easy and masterful deeds are simple, but they happen sporadically, and the consistency of the science comes slowly following after.

A NAME OF POWER

Those who have reached the inner Heights have learned, and now repeat as a song in their hearts, the

Name of the Highest, which stands among humanity for the Absolute, the Origin of Being. This Name was the heart-song of Moses and of Zoroaster. It's the Name taken up by all who lift the inner eye toward the Author of Being. It's the Name that the earliest known Egyptians had buried with them in their tombs, having the power of immortality.

It's not the full and final Name of the Cause of Being, Truth, and Spirit, for that great name is not yet known among humanity—it's not a word that can be taught. Our spoken words can only refer to a construct of the mind, an illusory being, never fully describing the Truth behind it. The word God, for example, stands for many objects of worship, and the word Spirit has many meanings. "These terms—Father, God, Creator, Lord—are not names, but terms of address derived from His benefits and works," said the early Christian philosopher known as Justin Martyr.

Sages have taught from the remotest times that we have the Name stored within us as concealed energy. The Name is within every mind and, if spoken, will be like letting loose the power of the atom. It is the Name that Jesus the Nazarene used, which had such omnipotent energy that when it was spoken it would heal the sick and raise the dead!

The Name that Moses heard from the burning bush, the Song that he sang in his heart for the rest of his days, called the Song of Moses, is the highest name human beings can speak at this stage. It refers to no benefits or works. It stands by itself alone. It is applied to no other but One. It is, in English, I AM THAT I

AM.[11] This Name, I AM THAT I AM, brings up from the deep wells of hidden strength that are in all of us the sincerity, boldness, and intelligence of leadership, and that originality of action and language, that mark the heroes of the ages.

Still, though I AM is the first name heard by those who set their sights on the Highest Heights, there is yet another Name, another Song sung by the redeemed: the Song of the Lamb.

In whatever language, however pronounced, it always means, "God with us." In Hebrew, it is Emanuel. For English speakers, it is JESUS CHRIST.[12] As immaculate as the name I AM, this name means the presence and immanence of the Most High. "In My Name," the Master Jesus said to teach and heal. "In His Name," his disciples preached, and it is written that they never

---

[11] We can't know what actual words Moses heard: he was raised as an Egyptian prince and so may have heard the words *neter neter*, but he had lived 40 years among Aramaic shepherds in the desert so it may have been the Aramaic words *Ahmi Yot Ahmi*. Or, he may have spoken an early form of Hebrew, in which case it would have been something like *Eyeh Asher Eyeh.*, or even the Tetragrammatron: *Yod Heh Vov Heh*, which is written in the Hebrew Bible and may not be spoken, although English speakers say *Jehovah, or Yahweh.*

[12] The name Jesus Christ is the English form of the Latin *Jesu Christe*, which is derived from Greek, the language in which Paul's letters and the early gospels were written. The man we call Jesus, however, was a villager in a country that spoke Hebrew for religious purposes and Aramaic in daily life. He would have been known as either *Yshwh bn Ysf* in Hebrew (which translates to Joshua, Son of Joseph, in English) or simply *Ishah*, in Aramaic. Both forms are also translated as "savior." The word Christ is English for the Greek/Latin term *Christus* which is comparable to the Hebrew term *Msjah*, the title of one who has been risen above all others, anointed as the successor to King David, who, according to the prophet Isaiah, was to come like David and restore the free kingdom of Israel, driving off any invaders, through the power of his connection with God

preached any doctrine except the power of His Name. It was their Song, and through it they worked wonders.

It doesn't matter whether Jesus the Nazarene was an historical character, a man who walked on planet Earth, or not.[13] The very idea of Him raises the consciousness of those who lift their inner vision to a higher possibility through Him. The very name, which can be translated from the Hebrew and Greek as "risen savior," has a raising power.

More, the teachings attributed to him in the New Testament bring a completion to the history of metaphysical science. No sage of the earth has ever declared himself any other than a seeker after the way of the light, but Jesus the Nazarene said, "I am the way." Appolonius, who cured the diseased and called back the dying, traveled far to find if Hindu or Egyptian priests could give him the law of life. But none could declare it; "I am the life," said Jesus. Prince Gautama, who became the Buddha and worked many miracles, proclaimed himself a seeker after truth; Jesus the Nazarene said, "I am the truth." "We look for one to overcome nature's dominion," said Plato; "I have overcome the world," said Jesus. "I know that Messiah is

---

[13] The fact that no known history other than the books of the Bible (including the various "apocrypha" or "hidden" texts) refers to Jesus or even to someone like him has caused many skeptics to wonder if the whole thing were not an invented tale, or, at best, a conglomerate of well-loved stories about various people. One possible corroborating text, however, is the story of "St. Issa," an Israelite said to have traveled to India to study and mastered many *yogas*, only to be crucified soon after his return home, which was translated by a Russian doctor during the 19th century and is translated into English in the book, *The Jesus Mystery* by Janet Bock. Now several books and videos have documented the same evidence.

coming, and when he is here he will tell us all things," said the Samaritan woman at the well; "I that speak to you am he," was the Nazarene's response. "I know my brother will live again in the resurrection, at the last day," said Lazarus' sister Martha; "I am the resurrection," said Jesus the Nazarene.

And in each case, he demonstrated his declarations with prompt proofs. He nullified the limitations of matter, healed the ailing, multiplied food, walked on the water, and, laying down his life, overcame death. Then, risen, appearing suddenly and unexpectedly, he told his disciples to "Preach repentance ... in My Name ... beginning at Jerusalem." Jerusalem means "place of peace." And his disciples went into that city to preach. But in order to do so effectively, they had to enter into the inner Jerusalem, the Peace of their true nature.

A NEW DISCIPLINE[14]

So we begin to return to our true nature, which is the meaning of the word, repent. Each morning, we lift up the willing inner sight toward the Supreme One, whose soundless edict through the ages has been, "Look unto Me, and be saved." We look to the 'Jesus Christ' within us: the divine ego, divine soul, our deathless, changeless spirit, ever present at the core of our being.

The Psalms say: "Therefore will I direct my prayer toward You, whom my outer eyes behold not, and I will look up. Early in the morning will I lift mine eyes

---

[14] At the end of each lesson in this text is a practice, prescribed by Emma for use on a specific morning or afternoon. These practices, combined with a continued willingness to re-think in the moment, form the basis for the discipline described in this section.

up to You." So, with the psalmist David, who became Israel's greatest king, we turn our inner vision toward that core, which is often referred to as the Heights, where the smile of the Comforting One radiates its Omnipresence, Omnipotence, and Omniscience.

Each day, and at any time that our peace is threatened, we turn our vision upward toward the Sacred Heights. And, in that awareness, we speak from the heart the two great Names. They are the only response the heart can make when the mystic eye is first uplifted, and only their sound has power within the uplifted vision.

We allow ourselves to fully experience the loving, comforting Presence of this Source Light. We allow these highest Names we know to flow forth from our mind in a chorus of appreciation for the wonderful Life that flows through and around us, from this Source of Being and through the comforting Presence of the risen Spirit.

And in that moment, we hold a clear idea of what is our present Good. We name that Good. All Truth is waiting for us to say plainly what is our Good. There is no spot or place where the idea of Good as ours cannot come. It must come and settle upon us. It must express itself through us and be absorbed by all the cells of our systems.

So we practice this science: each day, we look toward the inward Heights and speak to that invisible Presence. We no longer merely speak of Him, but speak to the Highest Self[15] over and over, for through

---

[15] The reader will note that Emma uses many phrases and words to denote the Source and Presence whose name we do not know—most commonly using the descriptors, God, the Highest, or Spirit.

repetition the mind is brought around to truth and the senses are awakened.

Then, when human nature calls us back from the mystical mountains to this body and this outer life, we allow ourselves time to savor the experience and contemplate the Good that is ours. We go forth into the day with a new life, a new wisdom, and new courage, and we realize this Good in every moment.

And again, should anything happen that threatens to disturb our peace at any time, we turn away from the situation and back toward that High Deliverance, feeling the One, and speaking the Names:

> O Lofty and Eternal Origin of All, I know that You are the Source of my Being, the I AM THAT I AM; and I know, too, that You dwell within me, as Emanuel, the Risen Savior, the Jesus Christ, lifting me from the pitfalls of my outer life into the eternal heights of infinite Good.

For so it is, always.

- Ω -

THE PRACTICE[16]

Monday mornings: Focus on Being

Begin the week by turning your face from all the things, events, and people that call your attention and, looking toward the Highest Good, speak the statement of Being, the Holy Name, "I AM THAT I AM." Name also the comforting Presence, the Emanuel who has

---

[16] The guidelines for practice are taken primarily from Emma's early work, *Scientific Christian Mental Practice*, which is a transcription of her basic class to train healing practitioners.

been called Jesus Christ by so many[17], who lifts us from the pitfalls of our lives. Sit with those names until you feel them moving in you.

In that mystical space, feeling the Presence and Power, name the Good that your heart calls out for. Doing so, you are naming God as you are prepared to experience It; you are speaking Truth, God's Word for your life, now.

> I am seeking my Good, and my Good is my God, because it draws, pushes, and moves me on.
>
> The Good that I am seeking is my God; my God is my Life.
>
> The Good I am seeking is my abundant health and well-being; God is my health and well-being.
>
> The Good I am seeking is my strength in all things; God is my strength.
>
> The Good I am seeking is my support and supply; God is my support; God is my supply; God is the infinite resources that allow me to express the God that I AM.
>
> The Good I am seeking is my satisfaction and joy; God is my joy in all situations.
>
> Life is God; Truth is God; Love is God; Substance is God; Intelligence is God—omnipresent, omniscient, omnipotent, because God, my Good, is omnipresent;
>
> God, my Good, is omniscient; God, my Good, is omnipotent[18]

---

[17] If the Christian tradition is uncomfortable, sit with the idea of a loving, powerful Presence in your life and name it. Some say "Goddess," others say "Holy Mother", others "Holy Father". The New Testament Jesus said "Abba," which means "Daddy." Gandhi said "*Ram*," Sadhguru says "*Shiva*," Muslims say "*Allah*" or call on the blessed prophet "Mohammad. Whatever feels comforting, powerful, loving, and "as close as breathing" to you will work.

[18] These words are suggestions, only; feel free to use whatever similar words are inspired within you.

Daily:

Sit down at a certain time every day and write down on paper what your idea of Good is, the highest ideas of Good that your inner vision holds. This repetition will make it more real; this process will deepen and clarify your understanding of the Good you seek — and are.

THE METAPHORS[19]

The Number: ONE

One is the number of wholeness, of unity. It is also the number of beginnings. It is also the starting point, a first impulse, creation There is One Mind, One Being, One Divine Experience of which we all are part.

The Precious Stone: Jasper, the White Stone.

The New Jerusalem, as described in the Book of Revelation, is translated as "the emerging place of peace." John's vision of this great and shining city has twelve walls, each with a foundation covered in gemstones. The stone covering the first section of the foundation is the opaque white stone of purity, Jasper, a form of agate usually found in river beds. It's also the last stone in the breastplate of the Hebrew priests as decreed by Moses, standing for the tribe of Benjamin, descendants of the youngest son of Jacob/Israel.

---

[19] Emma was a mystic with a huge intellectual curiosity. She read everything by anybody that might give her some insight. Numerology, the basis for much of the mystical work of Pythagoras and the Egyptians, was also a fundamental aspect of the Jewish mystical movement. So, while Emma's essential message is to focus on the inner experience, she often uses these other sources of insight to clarify her points.

The Apostle, or Power of the Soul: Judas, the Intellect.

The stories of the Bible can be thought of as metaphors for our spiritual development and each of the twelve Apostles of Jesus represent one of the twelve capacities of human beings. The name Judas means "praising God" in Hebrew. Though several disciples were named Judas, this lesson focuses on Judas Iscariot, who was Jesus' lieutenant and betrayed him.

The teachings that asked me to give everything I had or could get hold of to my religion promised me wealth of mind or spirit in its place. The gospels tell us that Judas was concerned too much about wealth: he was appalled to see expensive oils used on Jesus rather than sold for the poor, and he later sold Jesus' life for silver, which he returned to the temple before giving up his own life in despair over having betrayed his own spirit.

Shakespeare and the other writers of the European Enlightenment taught that the intellect was all we are and should aspire to, and that physical wealth was best used to enhance the mind. Yet the 'Jesus Christ' in me—sometimes called the divine ego, or divine soul, or deathless changeless spirit—is as little interested in my mental and spiritual knowledge as in my bank account.

So the soul-fire declares to the Judas-mind in each of us: "Blessed are the poor in spirit," for they are one with the whole of God.

The Judas genius is opened in us when we perceive the divine intelligence that pure poverty of apparent things is God. Possessing all as Spirit, I am to own and possess no thing. Lao-Tzu, the ancient master who wrote the *Tao te Ching,* taught that we must produce but not possess.

> So, through this first gate—my intellect—I let all that I know and all that I have been taught go free. I know nothing.

"The wisdom of the schools is foolishness with God."

Lesson Two: Remission—Negation of the Unreal

Metaphysical teaching is a process, like repeating the multiplication tables until you see how they work. Repeat them long enough and sometime along the way, if you've learned addition and subtraction, you'll see that multiplication is simply quick counting. If you're merely repeating the tables by following someone else's dictation, it may take a long time before you discover the core idea. But if you understand adding and consider multiplying, you can see quickly what's really going on.

This science of Mind works in the same orderly way: each step builds upon the last. We deal first with general principles which apply to all conditions alike, and then later with particulars and specific individuals. Your idea of Good is general; it's like every other mind's idea of Good. Everybody and everything believes the same way. It's in our collective consciousness—Universal Mind.[20]

The conviction of Good belonging to you is a general, omnipresent conviction, so the foundation belief, the first lesson, was, "The Good that is for me is my God—omnipresent, omnipotent, omniscient." And the first movement of the mind, therefore, is upward, away from the appearances around us, toward the

---

[20] Carl Jung used the term "collective consciousness" some years later, in an attempt to explain the consistent themes he found in dreams and stories around the world. Ralph Waldo Emerson referred to the One Mind of humanity in his essay, "History," which was popular during Emma' childhood.

highest principle, the highest understanding of the divine present in the moment, that we can conceive. Remembering that we are like whatever our inner eye is directed to, we choose to become the Good by focusing on the aspects of God.

Moses, writing the book of Genesis, said that the Spirit commanded, "Let there be light."[21] In the first lesson, we learned to hold the idea of Good in our mind—just as the Spirit's first action was to move upon the waters. The moment that this Great Idea laying silently in your mind is uttered, it brings a feeling of light and hope to the mind and begins to tell you great things about itself. So Moses, seeing the darkness of minds that were focused on the absence of their Good, said "Let there be light."

The second movement of your mind, after telling what truly is, will be the dissolving of any ideas that interfere with your experiencing, here and now, what you seek. *High mysticism is divine nihilism* and metaphysicians of all ages have made three great negations: there is no apartness; there is no evil, and there is no reality to matter. As they looked steadfastly at the idea of God, the Good, with their inner vision, these negations naturally arose to their awareness.

So the second lesson is negation, or denial, of the appearances around us. This is the second lesson of Moses, and of Jesus, and of all profound thinkers from all cultures. Even in ancient Greece, Parmenides could see, when he focused on the indivisible One, that all

---

[21] This is the second verse from Genesis that Emma uses, the second step in the creation. She says "The first chapter of Genesis is the science stated in the exact order of Being coming forth—as power, as intelligence, and then as substance."

matter must be illusion—and, as a result, his name became synonymous with leading the noble life for centuries afterward.

NEGATING BELIEF IN ABSENCE

Though all beings are aware of the Good that is for them, most people feel that it's absent from them, and they keep saying so. You'll notice that the instant you acknowledge that there is Good for you which you could be experiencing, the thought comes up that you don't have the Good that belongs to you; you feel that your Good is absent from you. It's called the conviction of absence.

It's a universal feeling: every man, woman, child, stone, stick, and snail feels at times that its Good is somewhere else than in or with it. People tend to think about how their Good is absent. They say aloud that their Good is absent. People rarely talk about the idea of where their Good is, while they frequently talk about the idea of Good being absent. They remain silent on the fundamental truth—the Statement of Being—that Good is here for us which we could be experiencing. This is how so many religions develop ideas that are contrary to Truth.

A belief in absence may take on many forms. For some, a belief in the absence of Good takes the form of being grateful that they are so blessed, more than others—but there is no possibility of being more blessed than another. Others are flattered by being told how much more they know than another—but as omniscience is omnipresent, there is no way for one person to know more than any other.

I tell you that all that stands between you and your Good, which belongs to you and which you could be experiencing now, is your own idea of the absence of Good.

The ancient metaphysicians who taught, "There is no apartness," hit on the most fundamental negation that could be spoken. It covers all the ground of everything we call evil, touching the cause of distress at its root. If you persistently stick to this idea, it can't fail to form a vacuum around you into which all Good must come pouring to fill you with delight.

You put away the idea of absence, separation, or apartness, the first time you speak the truth of your idea of Good. Tell the absolute truth about your idea of Good. Is there any absence of it in the universe?

Our Good is omnipresent—everywhere present, all the time. God, our Good, is Spirit. Spirit is free, untrammeled, unhindered, irresistible, here and now. To say that compels me to say that there is no delay in the way my Good comes to me. I need not wait.

When you say, with feeling, "There is no absence of Life," Life will thrill through every pore and cell and fiber of your being as you feel this Truth. It will soon be thrilling and vibrating every particle of your environment, as well. Nothing can seem to you to be dead or dying.

If you speak often the words, "There is no absence of Substance," your free Spirit will soon feel totally separated from the delusions of miseries that others may experience around you. All things take on an enduring Substance; you feel supremely real. Life seems real. Reality is the strength of your free Spirit that refuses to be mixed with anything like evil.

If God is Intelligence, then Intelligence is omnipresent, because God is omnipresent. Why does anyone seem to not be intelligent? Only because the belief that the human species keeps spreading about that Intelligence is absent from some spots or places continually deludes the inner vision. So you say, instead, "there is no absence of Intelligence," and as you do so, you may suddenly feel very clear and intelligent. If there is no absence of Intelligence you must now be rich with the Intelligence of God. You can know all things, now. And there, where the idiot seems to be, you see that the Intelligence of God is present

The great negation is, therefore: "There is no absence of life, substance, or intelligence in Good as I understand it." Or,

There is no absence of life, substance, or intelligence in omnipresent Good.

Nothing straightens out our thinking like looking at all appearances of evil boldly with the conviction that there is nothing but Good, and telling all things that there is only one substance, and that is Spirit; only one life and that is God; only one mind and that is God.

NEGATING THE LIMITATIONS OF MATTER

Matter is limited, burdened; matter is all the hindrance we know. Yet God, my omnipresent Good, is free Spirit, not burdened with transient matter.[22] You

---

[22] One way to understand this idea is to imagine being fully at-one-with All-That-Is—one with the Divine Spirit, one with all beings, in the Light of the Divine. As we do so, we can see no separation, not boundaries—and no form. Form comes of believing there are separations from that One, so matter is formed as we believe it is possible to be separate from God.

cannot say that in your idea of Good there is no absence without coming straight to the realization that all matter is delusion, built by some belief in the absence of Good. Say that in your idea of Good there is no delusion, and very soon all matter will appear as delusion.

The Spanish mystic, Spinoza said, "I choose to know Spirit rather than to imagine matter." Thales and Empedocles, the ancient Greek philosophers, thought so, as well. William Ellery Channing, who helped establish Unitarianism in America, said that since the beginning of time, in philosophical study, men have held that all is Spirit, and that matter is but an appearance, a delusion, having no reality. In the ancient Bible of the Hindus and Buddhists, matter is maya, illusion. These men could say this because their idea of Good was an enduring and substantial presence that could not fail and could not disappoint.

Matter and its limiting laws are the result of looking downward with our inner vision focusing on loss and lack, believing in separation from the Oneness of God. And by this constant attention, our inward vision has generated a fiction.

Matter is the appearance that results from our thinking that Good is absent, and takes form from our silence as to what and where God, our Good, truly is.

Because the human mind sometimes feels that its Good is near, and sometimes that it is far off, the material forms we experience are changeable. Even the regularity of the seasons may be seen as resulting from this periodic habit of thought. The collective consciousness of a community believes that sometimes its Good is absent, and so the region experiences cold and barrenness, and then the people feel their Good to be near and free again, and with that comes the fresh fertility of spring.

Matter, therefore, is transient and unreliable; it may be something that pleases you very much, or it may bring you darkness and great void, because of loss. So matter must be illusion. But the Good we are seeking must be substantial to us. As God, Emanuel, it must be constantly present with us.

So, does it seem as if matter were reality? It is nothing!

The reality of being is Truth, which is another word for God. As Spirit, God occupies the place that matter claims to occupy. Spirit is the substance even where the stones seem to be.[23] All life, all substance, all intelligence is Spirit,[24] for Spirit is omnipresent. So the bold second negation is,

There is no reality to matter; it is illusion formed by belief in absence.

We speak this Truth and the power of Spirit within us rises in its divine substantiality and every material

---

[23] Many current theories on the nature of matter, attempting to explain experimental results that suggest that the particles that make up atoms adjust their behavior to fit the experiment, suggest that there are fundamental "particles of relationship," which are intelligent, that interact to form matter and energy (e.g. Dana Zohar, *Quantum Self*)—or that consciousness is the web out of which all forms of matter and energy emerge (e.g., Amit Goswami, *The Self-Aware Universe*).

[24] Emma was aware that Mrs. Eddy's Christian Science teaches that "there is no life, substance, or intelligence in matter." She was concerned that this was inaccurate, because God, as life, substance, and intelligence, must be omnipresent. She believed that it was counterproductive to speak of these qualities as being absent anywhere, and so reminds us that wherever matter appears to be, the reality is Spirit, with all of these qualities fully present.

thing becomes subject to it. Our persistent declaration and understanding that there is no reality to matter will dissolve any material condition. It will cause a swelling to disappear if you look at it and say, with feeling, that there is no reality to matter. If a tumor appears to absorb the life of the body, it will disintegrate it to speak the Truth, that there is no reality to matter.

Whatever seems most real to you will be the first to disappear when you deny the reality of matter — and not necessarily in ways that you'd expect. If, for instance, cash money is something you cling to and you say there is no reality to matter, your wallet will begin to be empty. If friends are your idols, you'll no longer see them around (in material form). If you will speak boldly, feeling the Truth, that matter is illusion, all your affairs will be put on a new basis. Such is the power of an idea held as truth.

NEGATING BELIEF IN EVIL

The Truth is that Good is God and God is, by definition, omnipresent — everywhere present — and also is omnipotent — all power. This gives us two fundamental principles on which to base our reasoning:

- If Good is everywhere present, then evil is nowhere present, and there is no separation from our Good.
- If Good is all power, then there can be no power of evil.
- Can there be any evil mixed in with your highest idea of Good? In our idea of Good — omnipresent and omnipotent — there can be no absence, which means there can be no evil.

The only possible cause for evil is the idea of absence. That's all the evil there is: a belief in separation from God, our Good. The idea of absence from God and its consequences had to be called something, so it was called "evil." Then, since ideas always make conditions, the idea of absence, being held in form by calling it evil, finally brought forth all the delusions that people have experienced and called evil.

This is not a new understanding. St. Augustine, the great philosopher of the early Christian Church, said, "There is no evil." Jehosephat, the Hebrew prophet, said, "There is no iniquity in God."

The statement that *in my idea of God there is no absence of Good* compels me to say that in my idea of Good there is no evil. This is the bold third negation. To say

In my idea of Good there is no mixture of evil,

is to tell the Truth. It's a truth that will work freedom from all apparent evils. It will show that all evil — any experience of distress — is delusion.

EXPERIENCING FREEDOM

All reasoning has an effect. It controls our being and our perceived environment, so our whole life conditions change when we change our lines of reasoning. Having been trained for years to reason your life from the basis of Good being absent from you, you now begin to reason from an entirely different basis. You begin to judge not by appearances but by the Truth behind them. As you do so, many conditions slip away almost instantaneously. They were built up by your false reasonings, and with these gone, they have no props to support them.

If you have poor eyesight, for example, it became so because of some little notion that you persistently held.[25] You now give up that notion—you cannot help but give up that notion because your new reasoning makes it impossible to think that way anymore. The poor eyesight falls away and the good eyesight is restored. Sometimes this happens instantaneously, and sometimes it takes longer for the full realization to be felt.

For the most part, however, the heart dwells with grief on the contrast between its own lot in life and the bounty and happiness that it realizes is near, yet seems far away. Even while observing happiness, the heart may still cling to its misery. But to focus the inward eye on lack is to increase that lack. Specialists always multiply that which they investigate. Thus, between you and the attainment of supreme bliss is simply your claim of misery.

There's a subtle principle that we are like that on which our inner eye is most often focused.[26] For example, people often speak of how little they know, and finally others think so, too. The Roman emperor Claudius continually exclaimed, "What do you take me for, a fool?" The idea that others were not regarding him well finally affected him so that he lost his memory and did indeed appear foolish. Similarly, those who focus

---

[25] Louise Hay, the Religious Science practitioner who wrote *You Can Heal Your Life,*, says, "If I see a child wearing glasses, I know there's something he or she doesn't want to see." More recently, the work of Bruce Lipton, Joe Dispenza, and others has demonstrated that a change in one's belief can eliminate the symptom.

[26] In the Old Testament, this is "What you see you become." In the New Testament, this is often translated as "Where your treasure is, there your heart is also."

on the erroneous thought that caused a neighbor's distress will find it landing on themselves.

In so looking downward, we weep at loss and lack, while the offer has always been that there shall be no lack for those who lift their vision to behold the divine smile. The great disciple, Peter, sank into the raging waters when he looked down, having walked confidently upon them while his gaze was on the power-filled Master Jesus, demonstrating that only attention to the Highest Best can work the best into our experience.

Some people feel neglected, unloved, and burdened nearly all the time, and such patterns of thought make a region barren. Yet, while worshipping the Unknown and Unknowable High Cause, rainless Egypt became lush and rich, triumphing over all the known world. So, if every such mind rose and refused to hold the idea of the absence of its Good, barrenness would soon disappear from the face of the earth.

The reality of our being and our world is Good. With this Truth we set ourselves free from all that we could call evil. Does it seem as if matter were reality? We know it is nothing! Does it seem as if there were absence of life in some things? We know Life to be omnipresent! Does it seem as if intelligence were lacking? We know that Perfect Intelligence is omnipresent! Wonderful changes in your life begin when you reason along this line.

NEGATING DISTRESS AND PAIN

For ages metaphysicians have called the fourth negation the denial of sensation. They sought to get rid of the distressing sensations of pain, grief, horror, indignation. With their minds set on ending pain, many have been successful by repeating over and over, "There is no sensation in matter."

Yet if life were all delight and pleasure, nobody would have thought to deny the reality of sensation.[27] Sensation is sight, hearing, tasting, smelling, touching, which are, essentially mental faculties, non-material in nature—they are faculties of Spirit. As God is omnipresent Spirit, sensation must be omnipresent Good.

Spirit, God, is your sight, so you cannot lose your sight. God as Spirit is your hearing, so you cannot lose your hearing. God as Spirit is your skill in every faculty; therefore you cannot lose any faculty, or any skill of any faculty. Nor can any of the five senses bring you anything but Good.

If earlier metaphysicians had trained their minds to the high truth that

there is nothing to fear, for nothing is hurtful,

they would never have met with pain, or grief, or indignation, or any of the distressing sensations that all stand for the belief that Good is absent. *If Good is not absent, then the sensation of Good is not absent.*

Can coffee make Spirit nervous? Can rum spoil the beauty of God? It serves no one to ascribe to any item of nature the power to hurt. Nor to any human being. Look at them as glowing with the Good that is present in every infinitesimal point of the universe.

We can certainly point to the very strong ideas held by some men that their Good is absent from them when we see how miserably sick or poor they seem to

---

[27] This is another break from Mary Baker Eddy's Christian Science teachings.

be. The same is true for ourselves. We can rise from pain and distress the way Job did in the Old Testament, making the grandest protest ever made: "God, You know that I'm not wicked! Your hands made and fashioned me!" This declaration healed him. It restored his good. It brought him to even fuller experiences of his Good.

If you were in great trouble, you couldn't get help from God merely by begging for help, no matter how many times you've been told to do so, for that which we call God works only in Truth. Nor could you be healed by repeating your tales of woe: *there is no healing or illumination in descriptions of evil* — in fact, the description of our troubles multiplies them; it doesn't lessen them at all.

You would, however, get help at once, if you could stand aside from your trouble, knowing that it is resolved, and that you are greater than it. That's when you can feel the help of the ever-present, all-powerful Good.

CLEANSING THE SOUL

A lie must seem to be reasonable to seem anything at all. You would not believe an obviously insane person who told you your mother stole their wallet, but you would probably accept the reasonableness of a well-dressed, elderly gentleman's statement that a young gangster had done so. That's why, when great and learned preachers have stood in high pulpits and talked about a great being called God who made a terrible Satan to tempt little children to steal and lie, most people have accepted the plausibility of their statements. People have trusted their wisdom and scholarship when they were told that God sent His only Son to be badly used by the wicked beings His Father had created. But the whole story, from beginning to end, is false.

Such men have blamed all evil on sin. But *sin is only a mistaken idea about the universe and who we are in it*. This is all the sin that anybody has ever committed: being mistaken about their nature and living from that mistake. The Truth erases that mistake, and then our lives are free from the cause of any suffering or trouble.

Those who gaze upward toward the Good learn that it's a liberating act; they feel a fresh hope. They sense that they are greater than what has happened to them. They forget their calamities — and they are on the path away from the causes of calamity. Those who lift their inner eye experience the elimination of the apparent powers of life and death, riches and poverty, sin and virtue. They begin to see the dawning of Wisdom, and of Joy. Those who look to the Heights, away from labor and lack, find that their way is visible: "my yoke is easy, my burden light."

Pain and other distressing sensations are banished by the fourth negation, "There is nothing hurtful." "Facing Thee, there is nothing to fear, for nothing shall by any means hurt me," says the gospel of Luke the physician. All the hurting powers are nullified for those who look away to the Divine Original and allow the Light to beam from that Heavenly Countenance upon them and fill their senses with its healing Grace.

But no insistence that we are victorious can bring victory if the inward vision is still resting on the apparent misfortunes and liabilities of our affairs. There's no free grace acting for one who is focused on aches and pains. Our inward vision gives us our power, so no insistence that one is strong and every whit whole can exhibit strength and wholeness if the vision is still focused on the body's claims of misery.

The great British historian and philosopher, Thomas Carlyle, dated his new birth from a denial of all that held him in bondage. Through his life and teachings, the apparent evils of sin, sickness, and death had been very real to him, and he went through all the pains and consequences of believing that the Good belonging to him was absent from him. He felt poor and lonely and incompetent, and it seemed to him that the universe was void of life, of purpose, of volition. It was one huge, dead, immeasurable steam engine, rolling on in its dead indifference to grind him limb from limb. All at once he entered his protest. His whole Spirit-filled nature arose and said to the approaching darkness, "I am not thine, but free!"

So the fifth regular negation is this:

There is no sin, sickness, or death.

Where is there no sin, sickness, or death? In God, of course. Where is God? Everywhere!

This declaration removes any perceptions of sins that were put into our minds by our belief in peoples' lack of goodness. We shall certainly see people as more honorable and true when we have stated that sin, sickness, and death are not possible in a world occupied by Goodness. We shall see far less sickness if the idea of people as being undivided wholeness of Spirit is real to our mind. We shall be utterly free from seeing death in any form, or under any circumstances, if we appreciate that *in omnipresent Life there can be no death*.

BEYOND THE FIVE—OUR PERSONAL NEGATIONS

The Old Testament prophet, Elisha, visiting one of the schools of theology in his area, found the water so brackish that the students complained they couldn't drink. Elisha poured some salt into the water and it was instantly clear.[28] Similarly, many a student of the highest theology today has failed to drink the healing waters because his ideas were subject to what he believed to be his physical senses—and though he practiced the great general negations, failed to "salt the water," to deny the validity of reasoning based on those ideas.

The five general statements of negation apply to the whole collective consciousness of humanity, delighting the Mind, the Soul, and the Spirit. These five correspond to the five senses, but all five might be used faithfully and someone still might not achieve the desired state of mind. If we are not set free from ever coming into contact with sin, sickness, and death, by these five negatives, we may be sure that we have some special prejudices to get rid of.

The great Greek philosopher, Plato, achieved much by using these five, but they didn't touch his character. He rejected matter. He rejected evil. He rejected all that we reason against, but he didn't refuse his own prejudices. He had spoken of One Life, One Mind, One Good, and then spoke of woman as the failure of blind nature. He couldn't get the principle that there can be no failure in God, and no barriers against gender. He didn't know that it was as necessary to free

---

[28] In the Aramaic cultures, salt is often used as an idiom for wisdom.

himself from prejudice as from a belief in matter. Instead, he was always speaking of failure—including failure on his own part, and, in time, experienced the failure of his school.

Too often we see people who yield to some trivial temptation while thinking and talking this metaphysical Science. In such, the moral chords of character are out of tune. If you are careless about paying your debts, your moral chord isn't vibrating to some word of negation that you need to hear. If you use other people's property roughly, you do not catch the word that vibrates the word of honor. If you do things that inconvenience or tire others, then the salt of justice has not been sprinkled into the spring of your character. Hence, we all need to meet some special belief that Good is absent with a powerful negating statement.

That belief may be so subtle that we're not really aware of its presence. In that case, we must look at our lives to discover the results deriving from it.[29] For example, a habit of running others down will run some healthy part of our body down into disease, and, as we speak of all people from the standpoint of being Spirit, Life, and Substance, instead of from their appearance, such sickness will be cured.

There are two particular negating statements that each individual must discover and speak. These two particular statements address your own moral character and delight your own heart. So take two un-loving tendencies that you've observed as a consequence of believing in the absence of Good, and, like Job, tell God that you know they are in truth no part of you, because

---

[29] Werner Erhart, the founder of *est*, offered a similar model: he used to say, "if you want to know your intentions, look at your results."

God is expressing you as individualized Spirit, now. Say that as you were born in God's own Goodness, you have never had any trait of character that could result in the absence of Good. As God is never absent, God, as Good, must be here, in your own mind, now.

You may take a habit of scolding people far worse than their wrong-doings, and proclaim that as the expression of Spirit, you do not chide or condemn anybody; as part of omnipotent Intelligence, you cannot hurt people by your speeches or action. You cannot have a habit of jealousy. You cannot feel easily offended. You can't resent the way people act toward you. You are not envious of anyone. You're not cowardly about being blamed. You're not stingy. You're never glad to think your enemies unfortunate. And you would never feel discouraged when you've tried and not succeeded.

You see, too, that even the "sin" of being ungrateful for your possessions, or for your education, or for your lot in life as it is, melts down and leaves you the master you were when you first came forth from Divine Mind.

Now the thought that lies between you and the experience of your Good is as apt to be one of your virtues as one of your vices. Suppose you're very prompt in paying your debts and take pride in it, speaking scornfully of those who don't; this pride in your virtue hides the virtue. One day you may believe yourself to be unable to pay your debts, and if it causes you to be more lenient with those who are careless, you will pass the shadow that stands between your mind and its satisfaction. Or, if you're one who takes pride in never speaking or acting from impulse, and feel a sort of contempt for those who do, what you're calling your virtue is a claim to be something when it is nothing. Let that pride in your virtue be eliminated from your character. Take yourself in hand, and looking up to a higher vision of being, resolve to reason your special traits out of your character and claim the Truth of Spirit, instead.

Doing this for ourselves has a mysterious influence on the world around us. As we negate our special prejudices, sickness falls away from the people we meet. Death comes and looks into our homes, then hurries away like a dream. Sin falls from our neighbors' characters and they don't seem the same to us anymore. Our experience becomes what we have focused on: Wisdom, Peace, Intelligence, Supply, and Joy.

We do not need to wait to be free. As God is free now, so we are free—here, now, and forever!

- Ω -

THE PRACTICE

Tuesday mornings:

Study, reason out, and acknowledge the truth of the five general negating denials that come from considering the true nature of God:

1. There is no evil.
2. There is no reality to matter; it is illusion formed by belief in absence.
3. There is no absence of life, substance, or intelligence, anywhere.
4. There is nothing to fear for there is nothing hurtful.
5. There is no sin, sickness, or death.

[These words are suggestions, only; feel free to use whatever similar words are inspired within you.]

Then, find the two additional negating statements that are particular to your life, to be discovered, reasoned out and spoken by each of us on our own. Reason out how they cannot be part of your experience or thought. State them firmly, expecting the Good, which is your true nature, to manifest immediately.

Daily:

Look to the Heights and acknowledge the Truth: that as Good is God and God is omnipresent, you reject the common feeling of the absence of Good. As God is free now, you are free now, so sing the joy of liberty, free grace, remission, and unburdening. Join in the great shout of liberty, the high Pehlevi, the Psalms of remission:

> Steadfastly facing the Heights of Being, there is no evil on my pathway.
>
> Steadfastly facing the Heights of Being, there is no matter with its laws.
>
> Steadfastly facing the Heights of Being, there is no loss, no lack, no absence, no deprivation.
>
> Steadfastly facing the Heights of Being, there is nothing to fear, for there is no power to hurt.
>
> Steadfastly facing the Heights of Being, there is neither sin nor sickness nor death.

THE METAPHORS

The Number: TWO

Two is the number of complementarity: black/white, man/woman, darkness/light. In two we see that all things contain their opposite, like two sides of a coin. So whenever we are confronted with the appearance of one, we know the other is present, for within the framework of Creation, the One, Spirit, Good, appears in dual forms.

And when two are united in the One, far greater things are possible than when either stands alone; this is the "two-law." Jesus sent his disciples forth in pairs; one of each pair was positive, or yang, and the other negative, or yin; as, for instance Peter, the impulsive, expressive one, and John, the trusting, yielding one. "My two watchers" spoken of in Revelation are given power, they are "the two olive trees," enriched and set in authority, the "two candlesticks from above," filled with the eternal oil of healing. And with the sound of the second angel, the sense of personal responsibility, of heavy obligation, rolls softly away.

The Stone: Sapphire, wisdom & peace

John the Revelator saw sapphire as the second stone in the walls of the New Jerusalem. Sapphire is wisdom, peace, and health. We are building the temple of our own character through these lessons: jasper, the stone of pure thoughts as we fill our thoughts with the Statement of Being in Lesson One; and sapphire, setting free our wisdom and peace, as we negate the possibility of anything but the experience of Good in Lesson Two.

The Apostle: Simon, Zeal

The name Simon is the Greek form of the Hebrew *Shimehon* which means "hearer, listener, I hear and obey."

The second disciple of Jesus, and second power of the soul, is Simon the Zealot, who loved ideas, listened to the doctrines, and sought to reform others. He represents our love of sacrifice: the idea that we must give up something in order to be our True selves. As we grieve our sacrifice, we release it and step into our true freedom.

Simon is therefore represented by the Beatitude verse: "Blessed are they that mourn."

Lesson Three:

Forgiveness—Affirmations of Our Good

Now is the time to choose the power or energy we would like to embody in ourselves and to work at it until all its characteristics are visible in us. There is a Divine Providence always acting, always ready to give us something new in return for that which we negate and release.

Every objective we focus on has its own possibilities, ready to spring forth and fill us. We can take on any force by persevering in our attention to it; we can embody whatever we focus on continually. The famous magician of Samaria in Jesus' time, Simon Magus, was observed to levitate thirty feet in the air after focusing on the levitating principle emanating from the earth. St. Margaret of Paris became the embodiment of suffering and St. Francis of Assisi showed the wounds called stigmata, by focusing their attention on such images.

We also become like those with whom we associate. The British philosopher Herbert Spencer concluded that people are more like the company they keep than the people from whom they are descended. The early Christian writer, Iamblichus, noted that certain men had taken on majesty and superhuman capacities from constant association with the powerful gods.

Since God is Spirit, the Substance you long for is Spirit. Very well, be spiritually happy and the material shadows, the affairs of your life, must be happy! A beggar child, looking through the window into a home of plenty, who can forget her physical misery because her mind is so happy, and can keep that up for five minutes, can draw someone to her who can feed her body that very day.[30] So it is that when we know God, we have touched the very Substance that can inform us how to work each minute wisely, so as to be clothed and fed and housed and healed, without any other process than simply knowing God.

We can be filled with peace by feeling the ever-presence of everlasting Peace. Similarly, those who fill their minds with the third lesson of Jesus: "God is Love," fill their paths with delight and joy. And there is imperturbable health awaiting our identification with the Author of Health. Is a someone poor? They shall be poor no longer if they pour themselves into the Owner of all, the creative force of the Universe.

We must have our eye single to the One-Only in order to be filled with that One. Such utter yielding is called "meekness" in the Bible. As the needle cannot attract like a magnet if it hasn't yielded itself completely to the magnet first, so no one can fulfill the Great Promises who hasn't let mind, heart, body, and life go free with the winds of the Divine Breath.

William James, the great psychologist of religion, tells of an Oxford graduate who offered himself to the Divine Order, letting go of himself like a reed in the wind, fully expecting annihilation. To his surprise he found his bad habits gone, his despair dissolved, his character and body strengthened, and his whole being

---

[30] Given the difficulties of Emma's life during the Civil War, it's possible that this example is based on her personal experience.

infused with radiance.[31] "Whoever humbles himself shall be exalted," was Jesus' teaching.

But if we have occupied our thinking mind with what we shall eat, or drink, or wear, or other such subjects, we become little more than mannequins, lost in a dark state of mind — the Egyptian darkness of the Old Testament story.

Moses, who led the children of God (which is the meaning of the word *Israel*) out of that darkness and founded the Hebrew nation, said that acknowledgment of the right and true God (known to us as our omnipresent Good) is like a wind moving across the face of the waters for the light to shine upon it. Thus, as we begin to occupy our thinking mind with divine principles and qualities, we feel the glow of the Light from on High shining over and through the mind. Whenever we obey the call to "Look up," and "Behold Me," any opposition to the Good is dissolved.

So let us choose to be identified with true strength and might, with the all-knowing Unknowable. Let us fill ourselves with the Mystical Stillness until our tongues are awakened. Let us turn our vision toward the Author of Omniscience until we are filled with our own right knowledge. This is the forgiveness ("giving for-ness") that awaits us.

NEGATIONS AS OPENINGS FOR AFFIRMATIONS

It's no use making any affirmations until we have made the essential negations. All science has affirmation and negation; one opens the way for the other. In arithmetic, the science of numbers, you subtract what is not

---

[31] A similar story is told by Eckhart Tolle in his book, *The Power of Now*.

wanted from what is wanted. In the science of geology you say, "This is not aqueous rock; this is igneous rock." Someone tells you that sin is a terrible evil that God permits; you say, "No, God is the only presence and so there is no other nature but Good." You show as much wisdom by your negation as by your affirmation.

A young man who was seemingly very sick indeed, suddenly said, "Satan, get out of the way! God Almighty, do your work!" Now Jesus often called our belief in the absence of Good by the name Satan, and this young man had been brought up without any belief in Satan as having power, so he was only meeting the illusion of evil with a True idea.

A strong metaphysician said he could meet any lack of supply by a strong negative statement. If he was requiring money, he never said that he was supplied with all he could use; he said, "I do not need money." Thus, by negating the possibility of "need," he made a clear way for his bounty to come to him.

"Making the great surrender, Spirit Almighty acts on our behalf," wrote the great Spanish mystic, Alvarez de Pas. The One served by our inward beholding gives for our former nature Its own nature. "He that humbles himself shall be exalted."

When the right negations are stated, our affirmations are exceedingly effective. A powerful steam engine will not move a wheel until a valve is opened for a vent for the steam, so the day set aside for denials and negations gives the mind a clear draft for the finest affirmations to blaze in our daily life — the mighty Truth waits to move through the pathways of the mind cleared by the protests of this Science. After wise and earnest negations have dissolved our erring beliefs, it's never long before we utter the mighty affirmations that spring forth from the nothingness those beliefs came from, and our lives become consistent with what we now affirm.

THE POWER OF AFFIRMING

The One observed by our inward beholding gives Its own nature in return for ours. Today there are many people who, by contemplating the Healing God, rather than their own pains, have received vigorously healthy bodies in return for their diseased bodies, and buoyancy of heart has replaced their depressed thoughts. Their success denotes harmony, forgiveness; *they are preaching forgiveness with their bodies.*

Agreement is harmony, and harmony with the Adversary to pain, ignorance, disorder, leads to experiencing the success of the Adversary. So agree with the One who is adversary to pain, misfortune, defeat. Agree with this Adversary quickly — now![32]

A young person's ideals wait for their demonstration on the strength of their affirmations repeated daily; the tired mother who says "My God is rest," shall see that her thoughts return in form; and the care-burdened father who sets his sights on the heavenly "Well Done," shall feel his God take away his care. All the ways of life, with beautiful health, beautiful judgment, and happy success, are open to those who feel in their hearts the love gleam of the divine omnipresence.

The experience of prosperity is simply the result of acknowledging, either consciously or unconsciously,

---

[32] Emma is referring to a New Testament statement by Jesus to "agree with your adversary quickly" and reframing the usual interpretation.

the presence of God. Those who are prosperous have eliminated from their mind some idea that the one who is seemingly not prosperous still holds tightly onto. If you appear to be lacking, remember: there's a self-supporting power in the Holy Spirit which, when you let it operate unhindered through you, leads straight to your substantial support. People will think you fortunate, but it will be simply because you've thought on a high plane of provisions until you've opened a gateway of mind. *You must be satisfied in mind to be completely satisfied*!

You may take any position you like and hold on to it, until it makes your life demonstrate it. Declare yourself free of the shadow of belief in absence of Good. As that belief vanishes, you'll find you can stretch out your hand and lay hold of some new good each moment.

Successful men and women of all times have kept in mind their own strong affirmations. Sometimes they took them on as children. Rarely have they been aware of how important a part in their lives these positive modes of thought have been. Euripides, the great Greek playwright, was the son of a fruit dealer when he took on a lofty resolve and became a friend of Socrates. Virgil, the author of the Aeneid and the greatest of Roman poets, was the son of a baker. One of the Popes told of how he decided, as a boy working in the fields, to become the papal Bishop of Rome.

Even liars are prosperous when they eliminate a belief in absence, leaving a good opening for what they wish to come to them. Some people who lie become effective healers in the same way; they dropped the one belief in the absence of Good that the poor healer is still hanging onto. But, as we must reap what we sow, those who lie must get their hardships in some other time or way; perhaps they have an incurable malady of their own, or some member of their family is suffering.

If you discover yourself leaning on someone else for companionship, strength, or sympathy, remember Ralph Waldo Emerson's essay, "Self-Reliance." He prophesied that in the future, people would be taught to be Self-companioning and Self-strengthening. This awareness comes from the affirmations of metaphysical science: *as part of the One Mind, we are by definition Self-companioning*.

If people cling to you, it's because they haven't learned to appreciate themselves. When they realize that their own wisdom, intelligence, and power is Good, they will not depend on you for anything. Therefore, you must think towards them, and for them, in a way that turns them toward their own divine nature.

If you are one who believes that you are absent from your beloved friends, you will feel great satisfaction in the awareness that Love is never absent, because it's omnipresent. There will never be any feeling that what we loved and are satisfied with could leave us or fail us or disappoint us.

If you do not work with your mind as quickly as others, don't be dismayed. There's always one thing in which each person is quicker than others, and it's a great practice to offer glad praises that the Holy Spirit moves through you and in you so successfully. Rise and proclaim your freedom from the claims of your incompetence and ignorance.

The power of your soul, the all-powerful Spirit, Christ within, shows itself at the least little exhibit of determination not to believe in the reality or power of evil. *In every aspect of life, you'll find that the resolve to choose only the Good will create wonders for you.* Health will come plainly into sight. Prosperity is certain to come to you. Happy life, in all its dimensions, is yours.

You'll first notice freedom from sickness. Then you'll see how much better you get along with people who seemed before to be so difficult. You'll notice that your own disposition is better, and you'll soon be more prosperous. Many things will change in your favor that seemed to hurt you before.

So take a true thought in your conscious mind and say it over and over again, either silently or audibly, and soon you'll begin to look different as a result. Our bodies and conditions are entirely built up and moved by our thoughts.[33]

GENERAL AFFIRMATIONS

God, the true and eternal Intelligence, woos us with everlasting Love. Eternal Love is your Good, so to lay hold upon your Good is to be satisfied always, in all ways. This Love is not the selfish clutch of some human being upon our time or attention, our body, or our thoughts—nor is it the attachment we sometimes feel toward money, toward food, or home, or animals, or friends. If we should love somebody and then later do not love or feel loved, it's only that we have a thought or feeling of absence. This Most High Love is pure

---

[33] This idea is presented by Carolyn Myss as, "your biology is your biography," in her books, *Anatomy of Spirit,* and *Why Some People Don't Heal and How They Can.*

delight, streaming through life with kindness and mercy and gentleness and entrancing beauty, and draws, with irresistible kindness and mercy and entrancing beauty, all things and all people to love It and feel Its love. The delight that we now feel with a little glimpse of the feeling we call love is but a foretaste of the infinite Good that is ours.

The Most High Good is Life and Truth, as well as Love. There's a wonderful uplifting energy in the words, "Most High Good." The mind is lifted to ever higher feelings of truth and love. The Most High Good is higher than any we have yet realized. Therefore, out of the reach of our words, we have the Love, the Life, that keeps all things seeking it but never finding it, until the mind observes its own great plane of unreality and negates that experience with the omnipotent NO.

To know this is to know God. And we are exactly like that which we know, so to know God is to be God.

If you were found to be full of genius for writing books and understood how to write them, you would say that your genius was good. If you were filled with healing power and knew how to use it, you would be pleased, and see that the power was good. So God sees and understands all things in the universe and it is all good.

Doesn't it take intelligence to know intelligence? The more we can appreciate that the mind is God, and that there is only one Intelligence operating through the universe, the more that we know, in and of ourselves.

In you, therefore, is all knowledge and wisdom. By saying that God is Intelligence, God within you begins to show itself through you as great wisdom. You may be very wise in healing the sick. Or in speaking in public. You may suddenly be able to speak in many languages, as the apostles did.

The great words, "omnipresence, omnipotence, omniscience," will enlarge your sphere of action by lifting your mind away from your normal thoughts and senses toward the heights and depths of God, the eternal, changeless principle. *We silently speak the words, "omnipresence, omnipotence, omniscience," and we soon feel more powerful and wiser.*

So the first affirmation[34] is the first lesson:

My Good is my God; My God is Life, Truth, Love, Substance, Intelligence—omnipresent, omnipotent, omniscient.

These words have the power to put us on the right track in our thinking. Our judgment is better. We don't even notice that our duties increase, because our power to get things done is enhanced.

But don't get entangled in your own words—you are greater than any words you ever used. You are the mind that uses such great words to express your ideas about the Most High Good. For example, if you use the word "Om" to feel at one with the All-That-Is, you would be best served if you felt that infinite Om as your substance, your life, your mind.

At present, you use words to approach your own Good. *There will come a time when you will not use words.* No words can truly express your understanding of God: you are it—and what understanding of God you really feel, is the Substance that you show. So the only words you can speak and be identified with, as yet, are,

---

[34] The practice at the back of this lesson lists all five affirmations.

"I am my own understanding of God." And to say that I am my own understanding of God is to say that I am one with God, that

I live and move and have my being in God,

which is the second affirmation.

The third affirmation is,

I am spirit, mind, identical with God, strength, wisdom, wholeness.

This is our understanding. If we have called the one Being throughout All-that-Is, Spirit, then we are also Spirit. If we have called that Being that is everywhere Mind, then we are Mind. If we have called the One Presence the Universal Breath of Life, then we, too, breathe Life for all we encounter. And so we are identical with all that we have called God.

All who let the Spirit be themselves, as it is God, will sweep the globe with inspiration, for in them is the Great Spirit, which "sounds as of a mighty wind." Inspiration, or the in-breathing of the Holy Spirit, the Hebrew *ruach,* which the Chinese call *chi* and the Hindus know as *prana*, brings about sure healing of the mind; sure transforming of thought; sure healing of the body throughout; sure resolution of all one's affairs.

All who let the One Mind be themselves, as it is God, will speak and think the thoughts of God in wisdom[35]. There will be no slowness of mind, no weakness of mind. Thoughts will flow free and strong. Their thoughts will shed abroad healing. Their thoughts will

---

[35] *A Course In Miracles* teaches that the thoughts we think that we're thinking aren't real thoughts. Modern neurologists confirm this, saying there is a "default network" in the brain that plays the same set of ideas and memories over and over. Only when we shut this constant recording down can we access our true thoughts, which are in the One Mind.

reflect the divine Thinker, which can accomplish great and wonderful things. The world, which has covered itself in pain and poverty by wrong thought,[36] will uncover from its shadows of grief and sin by their thoughts. Now your mind, holding firmly on to Truth, through its intentions, negations, and affirmations is certain to cure any who come to you, even though you don't lift a finger.

The fourth affirmation is:

God works through me to will and to do whatever is my fulfillment to be and do.

Our understanding does all that is done for us. Once a woman held out that she cast all her care on God. She would never consider the possibility that she received her support from any other source than the Almighty, or that her life was assisted, or kept, by any other means than the Divine Mind. She feared nothing and nobody, because her God was her rock and her fortress. Though her childhood appeared to be one of adversity and misfortune, all the conditions of her life grew easy and bright.[37]

We are clothed and fed and housed and healed — we have all our blessings — by our understanding. We are free to make our understanding show forth great or small, free to make our world. We therefore make what we now experience by our understanding of

---

[36] "wrong" here means thoughts about the absence of Good, belief in evil, belief in matter as real, etc.; Emma warned her students repeatedly of the consequences of accusing anyone of being "wrong" or even "right."

[37] This may well be autobiographical. It's the sort of thing that authors of the time would do when they wished to make a point without drawing attention to themselves.

God. So the fifth affirmation is the same as saying "I am governed[38] by my own understanding of God."

Because we understand God, we love God and allow ourselves to be governed by the Good that God is. And, as we do so, we see that there can be no sin, sickness or death in the Good that we are. Knowing this, we affirm:

I am governed by God, the Good, and so cannot sin, nor can I fear sin, sickness, or death.

Those who know the unreality of sin do not fear it nor grieve about it. Those who know the unreality of death pay no attention to it. To them there is no sin, sickness, or death. As you heed the Voice that came to the prophet and said, "Say not 'I am a child.' See, today I have set you over the nations and over kingdoms," you will feel your transcendent nature. You can't help feeling that all power is yours to use. You can't help using your divine wisdom and power.

You begin to understand the Christ Mind, and in understanding, you begin to have that Mind as your Mind.

And when you have the Christ Mind wholly, you experience the divine nature that you are. You judge not, for you see that criticism is the result of not understanding others. You covet not, for you realize that your true possessions are wisdom, power, and substance. You live all the commandments – not because you are being obedient, but because they are the natural expression of your own Mind.

---

[38] The word governor is from the Latin version of the Greek word *kybernetes*, which means "steersman" or "helmsman." So, to be "governed" by God means that we are guided, steered, by divine Wisdom.

PERSONAL AFFIRMATIONS

As with the negations, there are, in addition to the general affirmations, two particular affirmations that each person must discover, deep below the surface of their normal thoughts and beliefs.

These particular affirmations are so powerful that they were mentioned in the Egyptian Book of the Dead. If you would use them, they would lift your life out of bondage. They are strong defenders and providers, being the strength and wisdom of your own life in its unique relation to all life. Once you have found your own fundamental transforming beliefs, you may add to them and explain them, but, as they are keyed to your unique self, you never need change them.

You alone can find and use them, however, for, as your mother cannot do your eating or breathing for you, no one else can empower you with the strength of your own affirmations.

You find your affirmations by looking at your circumstances. If your life seems turbulent, you had best speak of peace. If your life seems defenseless and unprotected, tell of the defense and protection of the All-powerful Good. There's no storm of adversity that can shake your nature if your affirmations are high enough to carry you over them. If you seem to fail in too many undertakings, tell how the Good takes the small and insignificant things of human appearances and glorifies them — don't look to the seeming failures of your life for your reputation but to the purpose you have held. Whatever has consistently caused you distress in the past is the key to finding the unique statements that will carry you beyond any form of distress in the future.

Meet the claim of absence of Good with the Truth of Presence. Between you and your true possessions lies only the claim of their absence. Meet the appearance with reality.

As you proclaim your right of way, down falls every apparent evil. Try it and prove your divinity, your true Power. By uniting our sense of self with the Power that we truly are, we are identified with our understanding, and all our noblest aspirations are to be fulfilled by being in full understanding of God. This is the giving-for that we have sought.

- Ω -

THE PRACTICE.

Wednesday Mornings:

On this third morning of the week, we study, reason out, and state the five general affirmations to provide the foundation for our creative power. We affirm our divine relation to God, our Good:

1. My Good is my God; My God is Life, Truth, Love, Substance, Intelligence—omnipresent, omnipotent, omniscient.
2. I live and move and have my being in Good.
3. I am spirit, mind—identical with God, wisdom, strength, and wholeness.
4. God, my Good, works through me to will and to do whatever is mine to be and do.
5. I am governed by God, the Good, and so cannot sin; nor can I fear sin, sickness, or death.
6. & 7. Your two personal affirmations.

Then we dedicate ourselves to our Highest understanding of God, releasing the old and calling to be forgiven in return, with words like the following:

Here is my mind; I release old beliefs. Give to me for its foolishness and ignorance, bright Wisdom.

Here is my life; I release old patterns. Give for its contrariness, true and everlasting Life.

Here is my heart; it lives in the One. Forgive its restlessness and dissatisfaction, its resentments and discouragement. Forgive its attractions and hates, hopes and fears. Give eternal Love for all of these.

Here is my body, I release old images. Give for its imperfection, Your sweet perfection.

Forgive me altogether. Give in return for my old sense of self, my God self, so I may be life and inspiration for all.

[These words are suggestions, only; feel free to use whatever similar words are inspired within you.]

Then hold the image of the highest possibilities of life that you can envision. If it's hard for you to focus on an image, write down just what you would like your life to do and be, and read it aloud at intervals. In time, you'll accomplish exactly what you wish.

Daily:

Every night, before going to sleep, give glad, joyous praises to the Most High, acknowledging that the Holy Spirit fills your thoughts with ardor, and fires your affairs to splendid achievements.

THE METAPHORS

The Number: THREE

Pythagoras. the Greek mystic-mathematician called three the number of Divine Law. The Jewish people have always regarded three as a specially complete and mystic number. Three is the number of balance and completion: where one is isolated, and two are in a dynamic balance, three is stable and reliable.

With the sounding of the third angel in the Book of Revelation, the star called "wormwood," the divine tonic, or mind-preserving principle, wraps the conscious mind in sane security. Ezekiel spoke of the third face of the inner divine as a lion, an emblem of strength, sovereignty, and princely achievement. We find the ultimate three in the Holy Trinity: the Father/Mother Almighty, the Miracle-working Heir, and the Mystical Holy Breath of Spirit Present.

The Stone: Chalcedony

The third wall of the emerging place of peace within and around us, is described in Revelation as covered with chalcedony, or copper-emerald, The chalcedony signifies awakening strength. It is the love stone, translucent like the opal, always gleaming like the purity of the diamond and the heavenly blue of the sapphire; the white light of primal Truth with blue flashes of wisdom and unchallenged peace, and the red- gold of Love.

The Apostle: Judas Thaddeus, Fearlessness & Freedom from Praise

Known today as St. Jude, son of James, his Hebrew name was *Judah* (praising God) *Thaddai* (open-hearted, fearless).

Thaddeus is commonly thought to be the author of the Epistle of Jude and represents the capacity to be fully open to life's experiences without being driven by a need for recognition: "Blessed are the meek."

The One in me is in the world but not of it. Loving tenderness and fearlessness that is free from the need for praise is the third power of the Spirit. We do not seek for praise. Instead, we are loving toward ourselves and others and watch the One within us who is not elated when we are applauded. One who is seeking favor cannot praise anything wisely: the supremity of meekness is being the highest we can be while not seeking commendation.

Lesson Four: Faith—The Foundation

The first lesson in this text was a statement of fundamental principles: it reminds us who we truly are. The second rejected whatever might contradict those principles: its axiom is "mind is as free as it has courage to deny." The third called forth the ideas that confirm them: "mind is as great as it has courage to affirm." This fourth lesson describes our relationship to those principles: why and how our lot in life is as it is, and how it may become what we please. The axiom of this fourth lesson is, "mind will demonstrate as much greatness as it has courage to stand by its intention."

This fourth idea addresses any doubt we might have that the Good is working to prove itself quickly on our behalf. Doubt can have a rushing and over-turning effect. You know what it is to fear that you aren't going to have things come out your own good way: this is doubt. It comes from thoughts you've had that hold God high above the world and far from your own life: you couldn't reconcile your conditions with that far-distant Goodness of God so you doubted that Good was shaping your circumstances to suit your heart.

The fourth strength of mind is the strength of inspiration, enabling one to see what must be done. The Master Jesus called this fourth lesson "Faith." He did not say, "According to thy denials and affirmations be it unto thee," but, instead, "According to thy faith be it unto thee."

Our way of believing deep down in our convinced mind is our human faith; our lives will show what we have faith in. If we feel confident one moment that all will come out right, just because a little appearance for the better shows up, and then our heart sinks the next moment because a bad appearance sets in, we are believing based on appearances, rather than having Faith.

Moses wrote, "Let there be a firmament in the midst of the waters." The word firmament (from the Latin *firma* and *mens*) refers to a firm mind, and we call a firm mind Faith. The waters are trials — as the spirituals tell us, even today. So to have Faith is to have a firm mind, even in the presence of trials.

Faith in the success of Good, even when some form of apparent evil seems to be upsetting your life, will act like a gallant ship plowing through the stormy seas. Holding on to the great principles while you seem to be in trouble will make your character marvelously strong. It is the very mystery of godliness. Situations are sure to come out right when people have a strong, honest confidence that they will come out right!

If you see a tailor cutting up a long piece of cloth, you know she will bring forth a beautiful piece of clothing from the apparently useless cuttings. This is confidence in the correctness of a procedure. It comes from having seen the process work. Similarly, if we see a sick child receive right thoughts through a practitioner or healer and we've seen the process work before, we can easily believe that the healing has begun, even before there's any visible sign.

It's not so much by what we do as by what we think and say that we manifest our intentions. Sir Isaac Newton was asked how he became so great; "By intending it in my mind," was his response. The early evangelists, Paul and Silas, held on to the thought of

God, their Good, and as they sang their hymns of praise, a great quake opened their prison doors.

Jesus taught that the only uplifting thoughts are thoughts of God. That's why, in the Science of metaphysics, we keep our mind's eye fixed on the one Presence and Power.[39]

While Faith means to be firm, firmness on the side of the appearance of evil, or opposing God, is more correctly termed, "stubbornness." In your thinking and speaking, you don't want to imitate those who say they have confidence in the Holy Spirit and then go on to complain of their ailments or their lacks. Look instead to your own relationship to the Spirit, and when anyone speaks of absence, distress, or evil, cancel that idea with, "I don't believe a word of it!"

As evil is not God, there's zero power in any form that evil might take. The person who sees that Life is God and is firm in that understanding will beat all ideas of death, even if a hundred-thousand doctors confirm them. Stubbornness to bring about death is not God. Firmness to bring out health, because Health is Good, is God, and as God is all-power, such firmness must win out.

Those who show firmness in the midst of apparent misery form the Infinite Substance with their mind.[40] As soon as you are certain that whatever has come surging over your life can't hurt you at all, the perfect

---

[39] Focusing on the divine when confronted by apparent distress is Emmett Fox's *Golden Key*, as described in the pamphlet by that name, printed by Unity Press and distributed by many New Thought churches.
[40] This idea is confirmed by 20th century physicists working with subatomic particles and energies: particles show up in the presence of an expectant observer. It's also how the Placebo Effect works: the patient's body produces the chemicals that the patients believe they are taking in.

condition shows forth out of that Substance, and things come out right. As Jesus said, "Your faith has made you whole."

We must have faith in the Good as showing our life conditions just right for us, no matter what seems to be operating against us—even death. God, the Good, is Life, so we are to have confidence in Life as the outcome, no matter how death may seem to act. Life, as all power, will win. We must be firm on this point.

CONFIDENCE TO COMMAND

In this fourth lesson, we see that God is no disciplinarian giving us hardships or deprivation, but is, rather, a beneficent Presence, awaiting our command. The prophets and Jesus teach us that by being insistent and firm with God, the Waiting Adequate, we shall find the Waiting Adequate most willing and competent. "Ask what ye will," It says in the silence, "What is your will?"

Faith, therefore, is confidence to command. Napoleon said, "The only difference between me and other men is that I have confidence to command." Jesus told us that with even the least little bit of faith, we could "tell the mountain to move and it would move..." Moses moved the people of Israel when he replaced pride with Faith. "Prosper me!" was David's command and he became the greatest king in the history of Judah. The prophet Isaiah learned that the Supreme Power is the most docile and obedient servant, awaiting our command, as he listened humbly in the sacred silence and heard the words, "Concerning the work of my hands, command ye me."

Commands produce results. Jesus commanded the God of Lazarus and saw Lazarus come forth from the tomb where he'd been buried for three days. And when he told his disciples to pray, in what is called today the "Our Father" or "Lord's Prayer," Jesus' words commanded the Creator to provide for each of us every day.

God is Truth. Knowing this, we speak boldly the Truth that the Good will always prevail: our patient will continue to live; our client's affairs are coming out right. If need be, we speak it over and over rapidly and constantly, so as not to let any other idea be spoken, even in our thoughts. We must be sure of it. This is the Truth.

This is so with the Truth about any situation. Tell the Truth about your child, about its goodness. Its goodness is God. No matter how much evil may seem to sweep over that child, be firm in saying, "All is well; God reigns; my child is good, is surrounded by good."

Tell the same Truth about health. Be very firm. Tell the air around you that health is God. Sickness is not God. God is all; sickness is nothing. Then be firm. Stand to it. Allow no other idea. That is the Truth.

Why should anything but Truth interest you? Why should what seems to be sickness baffle you and fill your mind with worry or even curiosity, if the Truth is God, and you have the Truth in your understanding?

So, even if someone appears to be dying, you may command the Truth to show itself. If necessary, go out of the room and out of sight of what death seems to be doing to make your command. In Truth, there is no death. Truth about Good is God. God is all-powerful.

THE KEY

There is a way to raise the dead instantly. There is a way to heal the sick instantly. There is a way to educate yourself in all art, science, and language instantly. Every being has a Life key and you have the skill to touch it and turn them to free life. As you command the Truth of Life where death appears to be, you will strike the Life key of the patient and that patient must live. Euripides, the great playwright of ancient Greece (about 450 B.C.E.) said, "One right thought is worth a hundred right hands."

Every one of your life problems has exactly one way of being dealt with, so as to have it come out right at once. There is always one key, one thought, one set of words, to address each situation we may encounter. There is always one chord in every mind that is capable of responding promptly in the cure of the one ill that threatens any body. It's only when this healing chord is not struck that people continue in their old appearance of sickness.

The more firmly we hold onto our own thoughts of wholeness and good, the more that we use conscious reasoning along the lines of Truth, our thinking will change and alter our patients' conditions, and our own conditions will change for the better, and then again for the better, world without end.

A metaphysician encountering a sickness that can't be promptly nullified has not yet touched the keynote to their own healing power. If a person sees poverty or grief that hasn't been made to leave the premises, that person is not to be scorned; rather we must realize that she or he has not yet touched the key sentence, the unique group of words which, if it were felt and spoken as Truth, would dissolve any poverty or grief and replace it with Life Abundant.

And we don't need to dress up our language. We focus on the highest and drop what we don't need from our statements — bringing forward only what we need to express for this situation, here and now. We put in the essential ideas — Infinite Wisdom — and leave out non-essentials — any description of appearances or old beliefs.

NO CONDITION TOO GREAT

The firm mind stands by the Good, focusing only on the Good. *The thoughts of Good within us must overwhelm any beliefs of evil that seem to surge around us.*

The apostle Paul called the thoughts of evil that make seemingly evil conditions surrounding people the "middle wall of partition." This apparent partition exists because between our thoughts of Good and our experience is a line of false thinking that reports ugly things to our mind. Yet it is nothing. Idle thought.

This "partition," is a failure to stand by the Principles of this science, and accounts for all the seeming misfortunes of aspiring people through the ages. They have supposed, in unguarded moments, that they must yield to material laws, rather than continuing to hold the high watch of the Truth of Spirit Present.

Did you ever say that you thought justice and right would be done in the world, some day? Did you think that it would be some time ahead, perhaps in the "end times" of the poets and prophets? If so, you have been judging by appearances, rather than Truth. You chose the words of poets and prophets over the words of Jesus, who said "This day is salvation come," as he told the people that if they applied his doctrine they would see the fulfillment of their words at once.

It's certain that when you put great words of Truth into the air, you may expect to see them come to pass at any moment. Notice the way the New Testament texts read: "Immediately his leprosy was cleansed;" "Immediately, he received his sight;" "immediately the fever left her;" "immediately he was made whole." Clearly this Science is one of instantaneous demonstrations.

Some say, "I can't help being afraid when I see sickness winning over health." Yes, you can. No one is ever challenged beyond their capacity to resist. There is always a way of escape from the greatest or least seeming evil. A person may as well say there is no Omnipotence as to say that they can't help what their omnipotent nature could throw off easily.

Others say that the alcoholic can't help drinking any more than a child can help crying. This is an insult to the omnipotent Spirit residing within him. It places that person absent from the divine power — which can never be. You must not side with the claim that anyone is too weak to resist drinking. If you did, you would be the weak fool that you say they are, for *we are what we accuse our neighbors of being*.

Some say the sharp-tongued scold can no more help her hateful words than a child can help breathing, because it's in her nature, born with her. Who told you that anyone could have a mean, wicked nature? Not Jesus! He said that all came forth from God. Stand firmly to the principle that ALL are strong, that ALL are well and you will see the true nature come smiling up.

Others say they can't help crying when they see their generosity and kind efforts insulted. What is that omnipotent spark within you for, if it isn't the Principle to be agreed with when the waters of grief seem to come rolling toward you?

"You cannot command me so greatly that I cannot work by you still more greatly," is the constant whisper of our secret Self. There is no fate that can face you with defeat. *You were not made for failure*, no matter who you are, nor how much you know, nor what anybody has told you. God, the absolute Good, is your nature, your defense, and your prosperity. There is no seeming temptation that is too great to be met with the Good and be put down as nothing and nowhere. The right action of the mind, when considering our environment, is to stand firmly in the Truth:

> I do not believe in a mixture of good and evil in the world, or in myself! All is Good!

GENERATING FAITH

There is a way to generate Faith, just as there is to generate electricity. It's very simple: *do nothing but speak the Truth and stand to it.* We speak the Truth about the Good as sure to come out in our life and in our work. We stand firmly to the Truth. And as we do so, our Faith goes out stronger and stronger as a power to drive back the belief in and appearance of absence, or evil.

Firmness is a mental quality that can increase our faith to the point where the whole world does as we say. It shows Good at every turn. It drops every appearance of evil. This happens because, *as we become very firm in Good, we don't give a farthing for the idea of evil; we laugh at it; we ignore it. It is nothing.* We are so firm, so steady, that we see all things as Good made manifest.

To generate Faith this way, we must be willing to humble ourselves before the Truth. Long before the time of the miracle-working prophets Elijah and Elisha, it was taught that we rise up with that authority before which we have been meek. Moses removed his shoes and listened to a bush before he rose to command millions: self-pride or self-consciousness is a poor substitute to present before people or nature if we want to command them — even for their own good. Solomon's choirs sang, "You shall ride prosperously because of meekness." Napoleon was docile and promptly obedient before his superiors as he rose up through the ranks, then his latent capacity as a general was stirred — and only when the success of his command led him into self-pride did he fail.

This mystery of obedience to authority becomes manifest in us as we yield obedience to the sublime by focusing on — becoming receptive to — the highest Truth that we can conceive. We rise up with that authority before which we have been meek. The apostle Peter was obedient to the bright angel who said, "gird thyself and bind on thy sandals ... follow me," and the bright angel was obedient to him, opening the barred gates and undoing the chains of the soldiers to whom he was bound.

This is the mystery of the gentle receptivity we call meekness: *that nature before which we have been pliable, soft, and meek, draws forth from within us its own kind.* So Jesus, the humblest of men, was able to say "All power is given unto me ... I have overcome the world."

Faith is a self-increasing characteristic, much as jealousy is said to be. A jealous person sits down and imagines a whole sequence of actions, then feels so strongly that what has been imagined is true that they act on their feelings and do dreadful things. The jealousy has fed itself by their thoughts until it handles them completely.

Faith in Goodness will feed itself and increase itself in the same way, until we rise and work miracles through it. We don't handle our faith; it handles us, since Faith and God are one thing.

We undo old beliefs in material cause and effect by replacing them with spiritual Truths. For example, you may not quite believe that the health principle is most powerful, but if you keep on talking about health and will not admit that sickness can exist, you'll find your faith coming around to the side of omnipotent Health.

This is why we often hear metaphysicians talking about not having a "belief" in this or that malady. It sounds strange, but is quite accurate. If they are strictly following the faith taught by Jesus, they don't believe at all in sickness; nor do they believe in any doctrine which makes sickness.

FIRMNESS OF MIND

Firmness exposes the very thing you seek, wherever you look. *Our firm belief in any principle will lead to a demonstration of the power in that principle.* This was so plain to Jesus that he said that one grain of faith would move a mountain.

To have a solid base of mind means to believe in something entirely or disbelieve it entirely rather than to be up and down with changing feelings. If, for example, someone in business believes in nobody, you can be sure that person will show no favors, so you don't whine or worry around — you stand up and keep your eyes on your own affairs. Someone in business who believes in everybody has the same effect, except that being around that person encourages you to believe in yourself, because that person believes in you.

If, as another example, you have set your mind to heal heart disease and are sure there must be a remedy, as you keep firm to that idea and seek ways to heal heart disease, your mind will get firmer and firmer until one day it feels a quickening certainty that heart disease is healable. At that moment you may be handling clover leaves. You give some clover leaves to a patient and he gets well. Then you insist that the clover leaves cured him — but it was the new quality of your own mind, your faith, that did the work.

While you kept your mind and heart intent upon healing heart disease, whatever you were handling at that moment will obey the waves of healing energy that stream forth from your soul. You might have been handling chewing gum at the time and it would have been just as effective. Then, when you have withdrawn your thoughts, or the influence of your mighty confidence has passed on to another realm, it will no longer cure. Similarly, all great remedies discovered by humanity have owed their curative energies to the continuous confidence of some firm mind. When that mind left the remedy, it would not work.[41]

---

[41] This may well explain how it is that so many medical treatments seem to be very effective for a time, but over a period of months or years are not so effective. Norman Cousins, studying this process, said that the history of medicine is more accurately the history of the Placebo Effect.

This is why our faith should not be set on the transient, material aspects of the world, but on the eternal, the Good: God. Our firmness in standing by Principle is our power, and *only when we truly believe that God's will is to provide our Good can we experience the true power of Faith.*

That power works as we put deep feeling into our consciousness. If you have been upset, you must put as much feeling into your declaration of faith as you are upset. The interacting states of upset and vehement words of belief will form a new basis for your character, a new state of mind, which has a great power. If we are trying to talk for health, or wisdom, or prosperity, and everything seems against us, then we must put great vehemence into saying: "I do not believe in sickness; I believe in health!" "I do not believe or think that misfortune has any power whatever; I believe in prosperity and success!"

Whenever faith in the eternal Good is generated on the earth, everybody breathes it and it touches their lives and unites them in eternal well-being, instantly. The New Testament says that the handkerchiefs and aprons worn by Paul, the first Christian evangelist, served to cure people. These objects radiated his confidence in his own principles, so that the shaky and feeble people around him felt his confidence as a brace. The Substance of his confidence took hold of the Substance within their own natures and recognized itself.

Similarly, when Truth is spoken to the apparently sick person, the Substance in our mind draws into sight the Substance of Good and that person is seen to be well. Yet firmness as to Good being the power doesn't make the Good happen, instead *it makes us see the Good which has always been here.*

CHOOSING A PRINCIPLE

The whole fact of demonstration rests on wise choice: we choose our principle, then whatever we choose must deal with us according to itself. To declare your agreement with a principle is to covenant with that principle; therefore, to speak a statement that resonates with your deep-down belief or intention is to covenant with that belief or intention. So agree with some principle and stand to it.

Then, to demonstrate the power of Spirit, choose your principle then notice what sentences, what groups of words resonate in your being, what works quickly to bring you into a feeling of power, and use them all together. Then speak them. Speak them clearly, and with increasing emotion, until you know, without doubt, that they are the Truth of your experience. Then you will see the demonstration of that principle unfold, as the Substance of your mind radiates through you and around you.

When the Old Testament prophet, Joel, recognized how few of his people had made their choices, he cried out, "Multitudes, multitudes in the valley of decision!" The great German transcendentalist, Johann von Goethe, wrote, "Choose! Choose Well! Your choice is brief and yet endless!"

And as you choose, you experience great peace. There is no turmoil whatever in the Spirit, and if there is turmoil in your life it's a signal that you've tried to believe in two things—the possibility of evil and the omnipresence of good—at the same time. It can't be done. If ever turmoil, or any form of distress, appears in your world, negate it immediately with the words, "I don't believe in a mixture of good and evil; I believe only in omnipresent Good." And if that turmoil appears in your thoughts, add, "I believe that only the Good rules in and with my life. I have the Faith of God."

A NEW COVENANT

Jesus taught that we can live by a new covenant: an agreement with Spirit by which Spirit is to do all things for us, and we do nothing for ourselves except to leave ourselves entirely in its keeping. It's not ours to try to change the external situation; we are to know what is true — this is our whole business in life.

This is not an injunction to cease all labor and sit and meditate on spiritual doctrines. We don't have to try to carry out this Truth by leaving our jobs, shutting down our factories, or refusing to eat. No, instead, we see that our knowledge is all the power we need to exercise and that it will regulate our actions; we keep swinging our hammers and balancing our accounts until our knowledge of Truth takes those tasks out of our hands. We don't have to shut down the prisons and reformatories, even when we know that in Truth there are no criminals: our only duty is to know the Truth about each of them.

And as we contemplate this Truth, we come to understand that it's not truly noble to be brave in warfare, nor to rise above the temptation to do harm to another being, nor even to be able to cure the sick or injured.

By thinking wisely ahead of those circumstances, we never come into them.[42]

You can prepare your mind with certain ideas and they will go before you like a king's guard, moving aside all apparent trials in your way. Your own radiance of mind, out of your noble thoughts and ideas, goes like a protecting fire before you and eliminates calamities, sickness, and the tongues of seeming enemies. It is the omnipotent Spirit, going before to guide you.

Through Jesus, the Christ Mind teaches that we have an easy yoke and a light burden. He had no praise for hardship or suffering, only praise for faith and freedom. So don't covenant with the Spirit for pain or suffering, lest you experience it. Generations of Christian saints have done so, and the Pietists (around 1700 C.E.), modeling themselves on the saints, told the Spirit they were willing to suffer and, though Spirit never asked them, nor anyone, for suffering, they got it. Their thoughts went out and Substance took form in their bodies and their world.

Firmness in our own minds about omnipresent Good is the foundation on which the original Substance of all things forms the Good in our experience. We give form to all Substance when we think or speak, and Substance does the turning and over-turnings for us.

The apostle Paul's letter to the Hebrews tells us how wise the new covenant will make humanity, how happy and free — heaven here and now — without fighting, or thinking about it, or waiting any more for

---

[42] There's a teaching story in the *Huna* tradition which asks, "What does the *Kahuna* do when he encounters a hungry lion on the path?" After many suggestions are offered by the students, ranging from hypnotizing the lion to giving up his life joyfully, the answer is given: "It wouldn't happen—the true master never encounters such a situation."

it. Like his role model, Jesus, he praised faith and freedom as the natural outcome of our covenant with the Good.

POWER WITHIN

There are twelve effects of holding firmly onto the omnipotence of Spirit. You will have life, health, strength, support, defense, clear thinking, wise speech, ability to record well your ideas, joyous song, skill in carrying out your principles, beauty of discernment, and great love. In addition, this Science of metaphysics offers the four main accomplishments defined by Jesus, the master metaphysician: to preach the good news of liberation from bondage, to heal the sick, to cast out mental disturbances and bad tempers, and to raise the dead.

All of these are present, now, within you, only waiting for your solid base of mind to call them forth.

We all have unlimited power. If we don't use that power with intention, it doesn't change the fact of its existence. Even if we speak of our weakness, the power is real, and demonstrates that weakness.

We all have a store of unlimited wisdom. If we do not draw upon it, that doesn't alter the fact that it is ours. Even if we tell how little we know, and appear to be feeble-minded, we can't change the reality of our wisdom, but appearances are nothing compared to the reality.

We all have the ability to see the Reality of things. We see Reality by being firm in our own minds. All is Good in Reality. The only thing between our good thoughts and the world of Reality is that line of false thinking (Paul's "middle wall of partition") which reports ugly things to our mind, convincing us to obey matter's laws. That false reasoning is the "no, you are not good," which faces all people in our culture, and when met by the omnipotent "NO!" of our understanding of the irresistible Good, it falls away.

FAITH MADE MANIFEST

Inspiration is the true breath of God. The God within and the God without are united by breathing, but the external breath of air into the lungs is only a symbol, a hint, of the true Breath, which is called by the Asians, chi, or prana.

All the ancient prophets sought and were liberated by this same power. The Old Testament patriarch, Abram, was working for the power of faith, and when he received it, the breath-syllable "ah," which means Spirit, became part of him and his name was changed to Abraham, Father of the Faithful. "There is a spirit in man, and the inspiration of the Almighty gives him understanding," said Job, having responded to the voice of God, "I will demand of Thee and answer thou me!" Jacob sensed the presence of the angel of the miracle and wrestled with the angel, saying, "I will not let you go until you bless me!" And he was no longer the cringing Jacob; his name was changed to Israel. Isaiah implored all humanity to practice this formula of the fourth dimension: "Thus says the Lord, 'Ask me of things to come, and concerning the work of my hands, command me.'"

The illumined ones of all ages have known that the will to command the Obedient Supreme Presence rises up after obedience to that Presence. The mystery of our inborn authority has always been the fourth theme of those who have, consciously or unconsciously, obeyed the Supreme Edict, "Look unto Me." The mystic law is plain enough, and Jesus, who mastered that law, taught us clearly, saying, "pray in this way, 'Thy kingdom come! Give us this day...Forgive us... Deliver us from any appearance of evil!'"

The musician thinks he is skilled at the piano because he practices hard. Not so. Instead, it's because he has, in some moment, accepted Inspiration—a spiritual ideal stirred in him—and has come forth. Because he believes he must practice to give it more freedom, this feeling leads him to practice. But the Holy Spirit is expressing itself through him, so it's not practice, but a free mind, that makes him a fine musician.

As we consider the world's most creative people, we often find that they've let the world's thinking alone. They've even, for who knows how long, stopped their own rational thought process—perhaps without trying to—and so creative new ideas and understandings have been free to touch their surface minds. Jesus taught this key to creation by Faith when he said, "Take no thought..." "In such an hour as ye think not..."

Joseph, son of Jacob/Israel, was in prison in Egypt when he learned to stop his own thinking for the Unseen Knower to touch his mind with words previously unknown on earth. This Wisdom was so clear that Pharaoh set him to manage all the provinces. This is the Wisdom which is ours when, as Jesus taught, we "take no thought," which is to say, we allow the One Mind to do our thinking, instead of listening to our normal brain chatter.

Let us heed the voice of inspiration. The lordship that causes the iron gates to open of their own accord and rolls away the stones from our pathway must emerge from beyond the three dimensions of our normal experience. It is from beyond the three dimensions, in the Faith dimension, that the Principle emerges which renders bars and gates of no effect.

> By past downward viewing I may have walled myself into apparent weakness, sickness, or defeat, yet speaking boldly from my faith-dimensional, secret Self, I am Strength Itself; I am flawless Confidence; I am Master of the willing God Presence of my universe, and all the divine forces stand ready to minister to my leaping Word.

- Ω -

THE PRACTICE

Thursday mornings:

1. Speak to the Great Servant with firm command, using the words of the Great Formula: the Lord's Prayer. You may wish to use the form you grew up with or the following translation:

> Loving, sustaining Creator of all Life, all-powerful presence in our lives, most blessed is Your infinite Name.
>
> We acknowledge Your Presence within us as a Power for our Good in all our experience, so that Heaven and Earth are one in Being.
>
> Give us our sustenance, today and every day.
>
> Give us Your Substance when we have failed to gain it for ourselves, as we have done the same for others.

And never let us be tempted to choose the ways of matter instead of Spirit, lest we become subject to matter's laws.

Repeat it fifteen times: fifteen is the number wherein the waters of misfortune cease to prevail against us, as in Genesis 7:20; it is the number of times the "Our Father" is repeated by pilgrims as they take the waters at Lourdes. So, as you repeat this Great Formula, become more and more urgent and commanding, letting your confidence solidify, and allowing the God-spark within you to speak the words.

2. Declare the Principles that you have chosen; this is your new and everlasting covenant.

> My life is the Life of Spirit; I covenant with the Spirit for my life, knowing I need not try to preserve it.
>
> My health is the Health of Spirit; I covenant with the Spirit for my well-being, knowing I need not try to maintain it.
>
> My strength is the Strength of Spirit; I covenant with the Spirit for my strength, knowing I need do nothing to enhance it.
>
> My support is the Substance of Spirit; I covenant with the Spirit for my support, knowing I need do nothing to earn it.
>
> My protection is the Power of Spirit; I covenant with the Spirit for my defense, knowing that, in Spirit, there is nothing to fear.
>
> My mind is the Mind of Spirit; I covenant with the Spirit for my right thinking, knowing I need do nothing to control or manage my thoughts.
>
> My speech is the Voice of Spirit; I covenant with the Spirit for my right speech, knowing I need do nothing to guard or enhance my words.

As with Job, my witness is in the heavens and my record is on high; I covenant with the Spirit to record my Truth, knowing I need not fix nor record nor even write my Truth.

My joyous song of life is the Joy of Spirit; I covenant with the Spirit for my joy, knowing there's nothing I need do to experience Joy.

My efficiency and competence is the working Skill of Spirit; I covenant with the Spirit for my effective accomplishment of all tasks, remembering, with Jesus, that "the Father within me does the works."

My discernment is the Judgment of Spirit; I covenant with the Spirit for my ease of discerning, knowing I need do nothing to improve my capacity to discern.

My love is the Love of Spirit; I covenant with the Spirit for my love, and I need do nothing to make myself loving or beloved, for all is the Holy Spirit acting with irresistible goodness through me.

[These words are suggestions, only; feel free to use whatever similar words are inspired within you.]

Daily:

Look into your life. Look it over and see what you appear to lack. Then tell the truth about it and be firm. See how it will come out.

Through the day, if you encounter turmoil, repeat,

I do not believe in a mixture of good and evil in the world, or in myself. All is Good.

Say it with increasing vehemence until you feel its Truth.

At night, take your hardest trial and put some denial and affirmation before it. Then from that hour stand firm. This builds your character in faith.

I believe that my good, God, is now working within me to make me omnipresent, omnipotent, and

omniscient. I believe only in the Good as ruling in my life. I have the Faith of God.

THE METAPHORS

The Number: FOUR

The number four holds the fire of convincing energy. It was the Uriel angel of divine telepathy to the Hebrews, the faith center in the body to Pythagoras, sign of the fertile square (i.e. "four-square") according to the Jewish mystical Kabbala, and the touch of fourth-dimensional strength. Everything about four was fourth-dimensional to the ancients, relating to the unmanageable out-side of space that renders adverse conditions of no account. The Magi changed the novice's name after the 4th initiation, because at this point, his nature had changed.

The Stone: Emerald

The emerald was once called smaragdos and was believed to hold radiations for sharpening the memory, even to recalling our heavenly beginnings, making us mindful, as the apostle Paul wrote to the Hebrews, of "that country whence we came out." In Exodus, it's the 4th stone in the breastplate of the priests, symbolizing the tribe of Judah, which means "Celebration of God" or "Praise Jehovah." In Revelation, it's the stone covering the foundation of the 4th wall of the New Jerusalem. It symbolizes our eternal choice for Good.

The Apostle: James, Confidence in Discernment

James, the son of Alphaeus, was also called "James the less," to distinguish him from the other disciple named James who became the leader of the Jerusalem church. *Yaacob* (Jacob) was his name in Hebrew, which means "supplanter." He became known as *Iamas* (there's no letter "j" in Greek or Latin), which means healer in Greek.

Initially, James was trying to do the best he could. Now he knows that all is done divinely well—he discerns Truth in all. Radiance of confidence in the new life that supplants our former life is not forced; it easily and simply forces the world around to come into order, conforming to the Good.

This faculty is order. It is located in the nerve center behind the navel.

The Beatitude verse for James is, "Blessed are those who hunger and thirst after righteousness."

Lesson Five: Works—The Word of Faith

There are four ways to deal with the principles announced in Truth. One is thinking deeply about them. Two is speaking them aloud — which we, as metaphysicians, don't hesitate to do. Then there is carefully recording the principles and their effects: writing down what we know about them. The fourth is living them, which we are sure to do, if we think, speak, and write them. It's by faithfully doing all these things that we move on to the fifth ability — accomplishing the works of the Spirit that is us.[43]

Demonstrating new situations by thought or words is called "works." The apostle Paul said that "faith without works is dead," meaning that unless some kind of work takes place, we haven't believed in anything, since all beliefs lead to their expression in our world and our environments are our works.

Whatever we have faith or confidence in becomes a quality of our mental character, and goes out to others through our thoughts, through our speech, and through our writings. When our faith is strong, we don't have to deal with many situations in the environment; they take care of themselves and let us focus on principles. *Works are the activity of faith, not effort.*

---

[43] One way to read this list is as the stages of development in metaphysics: first we study, then we talk about the ideas with people we trust, then we record our own experiences and understandings, and then we begin to live them, out of which we see the signs of our new consciousness in the world around us.

Our fifth lesson in the Science of Life finds us asking, do we believe that one Power operates through all things? Yes. Do we believe that Power can be understood? If we can honestly answer that we do believe Omnipotent Power can be understood, do we believe that it's worth our while to give all our mind and all our strength and all our life to finding out how to deal with it?

If our faith were small and we were to keep talking, keep thinking, keep writing ideas absolutely true, our faith in those words, which lies hidden in our nature, would finally come forward and make our conditions like our persistent ideas. Some students who have not yet come into their healing power have, just by writing Spiritual truths, conveyed a sweet healing, and after a while they absorb the truths and heal by intention and reasoning.

This lesson shows how essential it is that, even after faith has been established, we express our new faith constantly in our speech and thought and writing. "In the beginning was the Word ..." If we don't write down our insights, we leave out an important way of radiating our healing quality.

Sometimes a practitioner is astonished to find that he has cured a half-dozen people of very miserable conditions, and yet those cured patients don't speak of their cures or urge other people to be cured by the same means. This happens because the practitioner hasn't recorded the miracle on paper and thus caught the principle so firmly in faith that when a patient is cured, the fact is so present in her consciousness that she can't forget it and must speak of it.

THE POWER OF OUR THOUGHTS

Our faith in wholeness and good shows up in our experience as well-being. In contrast, certain religious beliefs, though it's not widely known, encourage the appearance of sickness and suffering. For instance, a belief in Satan as a being with power, or in the end of the world by fire and brimstone, has been known to make people experience illness. Similarly, if one has a strong belief in inheriting illness from one's ancestors, that belief may be the whole mental cause of a physical disorder.

Our faith also sets our mind to a particular tone, and when we meet people, they feel our mental tone with their mind. If they've thought along similar lines, they respond gladly. If they've thought differently, they may feel mentally opposed to us, but if we don't falter in our faith, then the constant sounding of our tone will break down the barriers of their opposition — as Joshua's trumpets broke down Jericho's walls in the Old Testament story. Those who once opposed us will come to sound a tone that is like our own, and they will be uplifted, and healed. Our mental conviction that evil is nothing real causes apparent evil to falter in their feelings. Our mental conviction that Spirit is the only substance will bring them into a Spiritual understanding.

The world that we experience is the exact record of our thoughts. If we do not like the world we live in, or, if we fret because it takes so long to bring thoughts of good out into our environment, then we do not like our thoughts. This is discord.

There are thoughts that we can love greatly while we think them; they make conditions that we love. This is harmony. Anyone who loves their thoughts greatly and loves their words greatly is sure to be a musician of some kind. There is much joy in their lives, too, as they continually experience the song of the Spirit in their thoughts and words.

This is because *thoughts moving in the mind form the body[44]*, as waters moving on the land change the form of the land. Moses referred to this when he said, "Let the waters be gathered together in one place, and let the dry land appear." After the mind has been firm in the truth, beliefs show up in matter. *What you believe will be plainly seen*, as the outworking of the law that's written, "According to thy faith be it unto thee." What we believe is manifest in our bodies and we cannot hide the evidence.

WORDS OF FAITH

Our words are clear indicators of our heart's beliefs: what the heart feels and believes, our words are sure to speak, and our experience to follow. So *all human experience has been created by our own imaginations, as expressed by our words*. Therefore, if you're given to imagining how something would seem if it came to hurt you, cancel that imagining at once, for an imagining is determined to come out some way, even if only in our dreams (for which limited experience we can be thankful!)

Some minds quickly translate their thoughts into actions. You may have a habit of fearing some little thing and it keeps coming up until it finally begins to seem real. For instance, you may fear that an old pain

---

[44] This, again, is why Carolyn Myss says "your biology is your biography" and is explained by Bruce Lipton's *The Biology of Belief*.

in your head will trouble you if the car is too warm, so you open a window — and yet your head aches. Now suppose you'd risen in mind with calm poise and said, "I am not a victim of headaches; I don't believe in them; neither do I believe in matter as a cause." You would have, by your very words, compelled your experience to be as you said. You would have been free from pain.

Jesus taught the importance of words in his fifth doctrine: "By thy word thou art justified or condemned." "If anyone keeps my sayings they shall never see death."

Our words are the outlet of our faith. As waters that have been released through the sluices of a dam flow down over the lands and make them fruitful, our words make our faith a working principle. And our words in the silence of our minds are as powerful as our spoken, audible words.

Some of the greatest lessons of God — in the Bible and in our experience — have been mighty demonstrations of the power of words. Jeremiah taught that a person's word is their only burden. Jesus spoke the words and Lazarus came forth, the waters were stilled, and the injured were healed. Then he told his disciples, "Follow me ... keep my sayings."

FREEDOM

Our word is our own to do with as we please. We cut our destiny and build our life with our words. *The one Mind, Principle, is so generous and full of faith that it takes for granted that if you say you are ignorant, you must want to experience ignorance.* We have the use of all wisdom by saying "I am wise," and of all ignorance by saying, "I am ignorant," so we would be rather ungrateful to complain about our conditions, especially as we can see that complaints increase the conditions.

There is no richer heritage than the divine power of the word. Could there be anything more majestic than the great principle that *every word is full of divine potency when true, but only seemingly great when false*?

People of faith walk through a ward apparently full of infectious disease, convinced that the power of God is flowing through them and blessing all they see, and come out without illness themselves and having healed at least a few others.

Uncovering the Real World

There is only One Mind and that Mind is the source of all thoughts. When we think according to these twelve lessons, or doctrines, our thoughts are Truth. All other thoughts are no thoughts, nothing. All other words are no words. Thoughts and words that are not in accordance with these teachings make thicker and thicker fictitious conditions: more appearances further from Reality. *We have exactly what we say we have, in the world of appearances.* And they are all subject to our Truth-full thoughts.

Yet the Spiritual, or Real world is not changed by our words or thoughts; it is the same changeless good yesterday, today, and forever. All our faith and all our reasoning simply open our eyes to the Real world. So we have nothing to do, for in the Spiritual world, which is the Real world, all is perfect. *The highest working power is the power to see that we have nothing to do.*

This realization demonstrates itself in our lives in many unexpected ways. If, for instance, we seem to experience hard straits with our business affairs, and we insist that it makes no difference to us in reality, this clarity may show forth in our healing power or in our own health, before it shows up in our affairs. For what, in truth, are our affairs? They're simply symbols of our Real life. Our riches are not material things; they're the presence of the Holy Spirit in us, speaking words of power through us. Reasoning based on that premise will demonstrate in good symbols. Step by step, our experience of our environment becomes heavenly.

Just because people around you may work out their homes, friends, and prosperity based on a belief in evil and the need for fear, doesn't mean you must do so. This is the one point where metaphysical Science differs from traditional Christian teachings: we do not accept the belief in trouble, suffering, pain, or sickness; we do not accept fear. Only our Good can come to us, for it is Truth. The Real world of joyous prosperity, plenty, abundance, health, and safety is our only reality.

The soul is the divine "I" of each person. The doctrine of the soul is that, while knowing all things and doing all things, it is identified with nothing. It is absolutely free. The soul doesn't care about money, business or bodily conditions, though it manifests itself as only good in all of these. To the soul there are no works to be done. Yet all works are done in the soul.

We cannot fail when we daily speak the lofty principles of Truth. *The Christ Mind, Spirit, within each of us would have us know all things, have all things without trying to have them, and be filled with power without long practice in science or art.* Jesus said, "the Father that dwelleth in me, He doeth the works," and "All things are possible to them that believe." We were not meant to fail, nor to be burdened, and there is nothing to do to be free.

OPENING TO THE POWER

You may observe that this fifth lesson begins to take away from us the management of our life situations. It's a great lesson in what Jesus called, "meekness;" someone is "meek" when they're willing to submit. In the Science of metaphysics, we are willing to submit to the power of our own words, and we say with Jesus, "Not my will but thine be done," knowing that the divine will for us is, always and everywhere, our Good.

It's human nature to wish to make others do what we think they should be doing. It's divine to see that their own way is their true way. People who hold tight rein over children often wonder why they are held from prosperity and good health. Some people hold tight rein over their friends, wishing they would do things differently — then they wonder why their health is so poor, or why they do not do good healing work. As we give all people absolute freedom in our minds, they will do exactly the right things.

Some people speak sharply of others for not going into the hospitals and prisons and accomplishing great works. This is a sign that these people believe God has given those others greater power than themselves.

If we feel there is work to do, we may be certain that we are the very ones to do it.[45] If we see, for instance, that crime increases, and we want it cured, we

---

[45] Emma's student, Charles Fillmore, expressed this idea as: "if it has entered my consciousness, it's mine to address."

say so. That very thought or speech is the signal for us to cure the crime of the world in the thoughts of our own mind. Whatever we may be doing with our hands, our thoughts are free to go and take down the hand of someone who is going to strike, or to lead a hungry child to a place where she will get all she wants.

People often wonder, looking at the phenomenal world, why things don't change for the better immediately after they have spoken the words of faith. If you've always thought in terms of things coming right at some point in the future, have someone who believes in doing everything NOW, speak Truth to you. As you remember that all Truth is NOW, your benefits show themselves to you at once.

Sometimes practitioners of healing can't seem to transform by positive, or direct, statements, and must, instead, come into their true nature by negative, indirect processes. For example, someone may not be able to make business affairs come out right by saying "My prosperity is satisfactory to me." Instead, that person may need to say, "I don't need prosperity; I don't need anything at all!" By insisting that there is no need, no lack, that person has affirmed the presence of what is intended.

Any act and thought, any feeling that demonstrates confidence in Good, will have the Power of God acting through it at once. God acts through confidence in Good. God acts through Freedom, because the feeling of freedom is a form of confidence in Good. God acts through tolerance, because tolerance of the rights of others is a sign of confidence in Good.

TRANSFORMING THE BODY

In the principle of mathematics, we get off track if we say five and three equal ten. God is the principle of Life; go contrary to it and you get off the track of Life. So, what happens when we think of material things as reality? Bodies, of course, with all sorts of troubles and pains. But they are nothing; they must disappear for the true conditions, the Real world, to be experienced.

If we were involved deeply in a mathematical problem, or a musical composition, we wouldn't carry healing power, but at the first note of the doctrine of metaphysical Science within our mind, we're filled with healing presence. Ultimately, when we rise to the highest thoughts we can write, or think, or speak, we see our bodies as a white glory of being, as transfigured by our thoughts as Jesus was transfigured by his thoughts. Yet he was not really changed; as Peter, James and John had been repeating the words of Truth he had taught them, their eyes were opened and they could see him as he is in Reality.

So will your eyes be opened; so will your mind perceive things in their Reality; so will your own body show forth its hidden beauty. People were perfectly astonished when they first found that there is as great intelligence in the feet as in the brain. Yet, there being no material brain, or material feet, all being Spirit, who would dare say that one part of Spirit, or God, is more intelligent than another?

There will come a moment when you comprehend how closely related your thoughts are to your world. Even mathematicians, focusing constantly on their calculations, change the shape of their body, and you, by repeating the twelve propositions of the Science of Life, will change your entire life conditions. *If you can set the coloring of your face to pale or blushing by your thought, you can set crooked bones or teeth by your thought.*

Clearly, we make our own happiness or unhappiness as far as this world of phenomena is concerned. You, yourself, are the arbiter of your own destiny. Why give in to the old beliefs? You're not obliged to believe that you, as a being, are liable to misery.

Remember that the world of phenomena is the unconscious mind made manifest. And this unconscious mind is, in turn, a machine built by the conscious mind. *When we speak Truth and feel thrilled to our very feet by a sensation of cool fire, we may know that our unconscious mind is shaped toward Truth.* Then we cannot fail to see our bodies and affairs show that thrill. The Truth will completely rebuild the mind—and the body must show itself in Truth.

Some begin to build at the brain first. Some begin at the bones. Some have actually begun by changing the nature or color of their hair. Some touch their environment first: even the winds obey their words. Some tell coffee and tea that they can't make them nervous and the coffee and tea become harmless—they simply reason that since our body is Spirit and the coffee is Spirit, all it can do is Good.

"My words are life," said Jesus. So keep some of the words of Truth running in your mind continually. There is healing in the Truth, whether we seek to be healed or not. There is power and beautiful prosperity in the Truth, whether we ask for them or not. It works through us like a fine fire of sweetness. So let us fill our minds with thoughts of Truth each day.

- Ω -

THE PRACTICE

Friday mornings:

On this fifth morning, we focus on speaking the Word and allowing the works of Truth to unfold in our lives.

> As Divine Mind, which I am,
>
> I preach the gospel,
>
> I heal the sick,
>
> I cast out demonic passions, and
>
> I raise the dead.
>
> I work the works of Good, so divine power works through me and as me to will and do what is mine to do, according to the teachings of Jesus: "The words that I speak unto you, I speak not of myself, but the Loving Creator that dwells in me does the works."

Daily:

Keep some of the words of Truth running in your mind continually; they reconstruct the mind along the lines of Truth, and the environment must follow.

THE METAPHORS

The Number: FIVE

Five was a living number to the ancient Hebrews: it signified The Representative. Jacob/Israel's son Joseph was the Representative of the Pharaoh, Jesus represented God the Father to his disciples. Such representatives, or deputies, must wait for the authority to act, so Five is the number of expectation, or hesitancy to act.

Five is also the number of redemption—it took five oxen to redeem a thief who had stolen one; it took five stones in David's sling to redeem Israel from Goliath of the Philistines, Jesus took five loaves to redeem the hunger of the five thousand, and so forth. All work is redemption, as well, redeeming a place or a people or a situation from one situation from one status to another.

So the Fifth lesson is a working doctrine: vision works on the mind; mind works on the body; in five, all labor is successful. When the fifth angel sounds, the senses are darkened so that God can be experienced.

The Stone: Sardonyx

The "shining stone" sardonyx is the stone of understanding, and the tribe of Israel whose stone this is in the high priest's vestment, is Issachar. It is the stone of representation, bearing the seal of the Pharaoh and the words "I depute." In the body, it represents the energy center of power at the solar plexus. The fifth wall of the New Jerusalem shines with the understanding of the sardonyx.

The Apostle: Thomas, a Fool for the Christ

Thomas Didymus is the Greek name telling us that this disciple was a twin. The Hebrew name is Ta-om Judah, which translates into English as Judas the Twin. His double name indicates that he may have been a twin of one of the disciples—even, some say, of Jesus.

From the gospel story of Thomas' unwillingness to believe Jesus' resurrection until he saw the holes in his hands, feet, and side, we get the phrase "Doubting Thomas."

The Beatitude associated with Thomas is, "Blessed are the merciful," and Thomas is the reminder that the divine is always merciful — even when we disbelieve.[46]

---

[46] The Gnostic *Gospel of Thomas*, discovered near the ancient monastery at *Nag Hammadi* in Egypt, is a list of sayings attributed to Jesus, many of which overlap the sayings in the traditional four gospels, but some of which are far more mystical in tone and content, many saying almost exactly what Emma is saying here.

Lesson Six. Understanding the Secret of the Lord

Of the teachings offered on earth now, this Science is closest to the initial Christian doctrine, but there are some words yet to be spoken. There is a secret not yet revealed to humanity, even in this Science, thus far. We can tell this is so, because we are not yet doing all the works done by the Master Jesus.

In the fifth lesson, we learned the Law of the Word. Through this law our word carries faith into immediate and irresistible action, or works. Unfortunately, many people keep their faith so hidden that it doesn't work outwardly. Others, like the great American Transcendentalist, Ralph Waldo Emerson, have used the Law of the Word, but not consistently. Emerson spoke of the unreality of evil, and of the omnipresence of God, but he also said that the gods overload with disadvantages those whom they would compel to do mighty tasks. He said this so powerfully that it affected his life: he lost his wife and son and had to overcome great opposition; ultimately, he experienced a strange loss of mental faculties. This was his own overloading, as he had spoken it.

Moses told his people to keep all of the words of the covenant with God, and do them, that they might be prospered in all their undertakings. Notice how this parallels our lessons thus far: the covenant first (lesson 4), then keep the words (lesson 5), then prosperity, which we define as the powers of the Spirit, remembering that Jesus called our abundant prosperity, "the

Kingdom of Heaven." The word is a pathway to the power of God. And this power is the sixth lesson.

THE POWER REVEALED

This sixth lesson deals with the Secret of the quickening power of the Spirit in our understanding. *We must practice this Science, this way of knowing, to discover the Secret.* We must rouse our whole being and, as Spirit, declare that we do understand the Secret of the Lord concerning life, health, strength, support, and defense, without material means. We do so as Spirit, recognizing that we *are* Spirit, and Spirit is all Wisdom, all Intelligence, for all time. Jesus the Nazarene gave this Secret to the world when the Spirit spoke through him, saying, "Abide in Me..." "Keep my words..." "The Comforter will come in my name."

Some people win their way nearly everywhere they go. A doctor who worked in Denver, in the "Old West," is said to have always spoken so encouragingly to his patients that every family liked to have him enter their house, because he radiated courage and buoyancy. He always told people, even near death, that there was no reason why they shouldn't get well right away. It might be said that he lost some of these cases, but their loss didn't seem to affect his practice at all, because other doctors who looked melancholy and hopeless lost more than he.

His constant affirmation to his patients, "You'll get well; you're better off than you've been imagining," finally became his whole mental state, and his presence radiated it like sunshine. He had no high standing in school, but the drugs he administered had more healing qualities than the drugs given out by other, more studious doctors. It was his independent mind, shining by its own convictions, that spread the healing. Had he been swayed from his own idea to others by his fellow-physicians, studying their shadow-system of drug usage, he would have been more like what he read in their books, and much less like himself.

Some people don't seem beautiful to look at, but still uplift us and command our admiration, even while they do or say very little. It's said that when the great Civil War hero, General Butler, entered a room or restaurant, even where nobody knew who he was, something about his presence attracted attention, and people were convinced that here was a strong and great man.

Some people achieve results even when others insist it's impossible. A man on a desert island kept saying, "Living Water!" while his companions mourned over their thirst. There was no visible water there, but still he kept saying "Living Water." Finally, he felt he must dig for water in a certain spot. The others laughed, but he persisted in spite of their jeers, and he struck a spring of water so powerful that they had to pull him out quickly, or he would have drowned.

It was the same for the fishermen who obeyed Jesus and cast their nets on the right side of the boat. It will be the same for us if we persist in the high way of thinking, keep speaking high and noble Truth.

WHAT'S HAPPENING, HERE?

There comes a moment when the full power of the words comes surging through us. The power comes through the words, and the power is the Kingdom of God. As Paul, the early Christian evangelist said, "The Kingdom of

God is not in word but in Power." It's through the use of right words that the devoted come into their demonstration of power. And Mohini Chatterji, the great translator of the Hindu sacred scripture, *The Bhagavad Gita*, said, "The powers of Deity are beyond description and enumeration, yet both description and enumeration are needed for the benefit of the devoted."

ACKNOWLEDGING THE GIFT

You'll notice a great difference in your power if you say that everything we call good that happens in your life is a demonstration of the presence of the Holy Spirit working in your life. Your acknowledgment of the Spirit will affect you mysteriously, altering your apparent relationship to the Good.

A Japanese youth, Kurozumi Saki, found himself gifted with miraculous healing power through constant praise of Deity for all his blessings. It took several years to accomplish it, but he did it, and was cured of consumption in its worst form by that one practice. The Power of God came into him, called by some the Holy Spirit, and by others, Understanding.

Maybe you think your life is so miserable that you can't be thankful. That can't be true, under any circumstances! Jesus always gave thanks before he wrought a miracle. Even when it appeared there was nothing to be thankful for, as when his good friend Lazarus was buried in a tomb, Jesus felt the gift of God stirred up in him, and this gift was roused to its highest power

"God saw that it was good." God is Mind. Mind sees that all is Good. What it sees and smells and tastes is Good. Nothing hurts. Nothing offends. This is the power of the covenant kept with God. Those who covenant with death, receive death. The Old Testament prophet, Isaiah, prophesied that sometime, the "covenant with death shall be annulled and the agreement with hell shall not stand." All the garbage of lies shall be swept away. Then comes prosperity, the "Kingdom of Heaven." Nobody need strive or haste for prosperity if their faith is fixed and words keep repeating this covenant.

The great 18th century Swedish engineer, writer, and mystic, Imanuel Swedenborg, said that the angels looking at us see only good in us: "our evil they behold not." It is to this absent evil and present good that the study of the Divine Mind, through this metaphysical Science, brings us.

A lady had been treating a patient with sore eyes for a long time. One day she had an idea, and impetuously spoke it in her thoughts, "You, as Spirit, have no bad temper!" The next day the patient came in, all cured. She said that sometimes, after weeks of working with a case, she would suddenly think, "You never could, as a spiritual being, feel dissatisfied with your son!" Or, "You, as Spirit, can say that you, as spirit, cannot be unjust with anybody!" These sudden thoughts seemed to cut a tough thread that was binding the patient's mind to an idea of illness. They were the key that touched the chord of the patient and allowed the Spirit to become manifest as Health.

While we see good, we are powerful, but the instant we see something to fear, we are paralyzed by the darkness of our own thought. It is prophesied in Revelation that all shall be light sometime — this is the state of mind that sees all things good.

THE SOUL'S SCIENCE

There are two standpoints from which to look at the propositions of this Science. One is the material, or human, and the other is the spiritual. One is unreal and the other, Real. One is our Adam nature, our intellect, with its erroneous ideas about life and God, naming all things by material names and living in fear. The other is our Christ nature, with its faith-full ideas of God and life, bringing forth a capable, fearless mind.

We all hold unexpressed faith — in either Spirit or in matter. Yet since there is, in Truth, no matter, there can be no science of matter, and *whoever seeks cause or cure in the study of matter must therefore be forever baffled.* Only in the science of Substance can cause and cure be found. Therefore, all sciences must be one Science: the science of Life must be the science of Substance, must be the science of Spirit.[47]

And, like all sciences, this one must be studied for itself. A mathematician who studies mathematics in order to get an appointment at a university will not be a successful mathematician; the work of such a person is superficial and external. Shall the science of Spirit be less exacting?

We need to trace our logic to its deepest practical outcome, finding, in thought and words, the springs of Truth beneath them, until those truths are externalized.

As far back as the earliest teachings of the Buddha, we are taught that it's our part in life to stand aside and let the Spirit within work for us. We do not fast in order

---

[47] Even the great 20th century physicist, Albert Einstein, acknowledged this when he said, "I'm only interested in the thoughts of God..." and "Science without religion is lame; religion without science is blind."

to become spiritual, but we may find ourselves fasting because we are spiritual. One does not speak true words in order to become spiritual, but because she is spiritual.

The pure Truth is spoken as itself, not as what it is commanded to do by our Adam nature, which is the shadow of our true, Christ nature. If one is studying this Science for the sake of one's body, business, or intellect, one's words are like shells filled only with desire.

Such people will soon discover that this Science is to be studied for its own sake, that its ministry will bring them its gifts in its own order at its own judgment. They'll come to understand that this Science is not a new way to make money, nor a new pill, nor a new trick for increasing intellectual capacity. It's a means for expressing our true nature.

There has always been a teaching in the world that there is a kingdom of beauty and goodness near at hand. And, now and then in the wilderness spots of this earth, sights and sounds are experienced that prove that the less our mind, with its earthly descriptions of life and love, touches anybody or anything, the more we may see of heavenly things.

How to experience this place consistently has been the mystery. People have fasted and prayed and limited themselves in every way in order to see it, yet still it seemed far off.

Jesus, however, always walked there. Jesus knew that here, in our midst, abides the glory of God. Jesus called it, "the Kingdom of Heaven." Here, all is good.

This is the new way of thinking that now comes with this Science. It opens our eyes to see things as they truly are, so that, right where we are now, we may work miracles.

Moses said, "Stand and see thy salvation." We begin to see the world at its best, step by step. At each purer realization, the world takes a different turn in appearances.

As the lily looks different at night from the same lily seen in the daylight, so this world looks very different in the nighttime of human thought from that great and glorious world which is our true inheritance.

Intellectuals call this idealism,[48] or transcendentalism, saying all who think this way strive to achieve impossible ideals. But the mind dominated by intellect and matter is constantly placing limitation, even on the power of God.

Have you ever heard a doctor saying that a sick child must die? Did you ever hear of Jesus saying that a child must die?

Those who feel most in their minds the Christ Mind of Jesus think most about the presence of Life. They do not agree with intellect or matter; they go to the child, now, and cure her. They know only unlimited, unhindered, spiritual vitality, force, health, provision, and protection, here and now. They experience it by the union of their human minds with the Mind that is God. This is the practice of transcendentalist teachings. This is the true Science.

---

[48] The official term for this philosophy is "monistic idealism," sometimes called "Neoplatonism," because Plato insisted that an ideal form of everything existed and that only our thoughts prevent us from seeing that ideal. "Neoplatonism" was extended in the Christian world by the early writer Plotinus, who declared, as Emma does, that all is Spirit.

FOCUS & DISCERNMENT

This is not a science of right thinking or of right conduct; those are strenuous labors. This is the science whose *results* show up as good or bad thought or conduct—it's the science of the origins of both conduct and thoughts.

There are ways of handling our thoughts quite independently of what seems to be going on, or of the opinions of others. Thinking independently, according to your own convictions, will make others see your lofty soul—not that you are doing so for the sake of their respect and attention, but as you focus on noble ideas for their own sake, you will become a radiant expression of the Principle behind them.

It's never too late to begin handling one's thoughts, even if you're seventy or eighty years of age, as the world counts it. You will need a systematic pattern of reasoning that has power to enliven you to a higher, bright, and clear understanding of Principle. And it's your nature—the nature of every mind—to choose to focus on the greatest ideas, once those ideas have been introduced.

The Bible was translated as telling us to "fear the Lord." The term that has been translated as "fear" means "singleness of eye." "In the fear of the Lord is the instruction of wisdom." Such "fear," or singleness of eye, toward any objective, must lead to the disclosure of its secrets as well as the experience of its working power.

Focusing on Principle enables us to quickly distinguish what will manifest as good from what won't. Paul said, "I had not known sin but by the law," when he found how quickly his new understanding led him to detect the error of his thoughts.

Your discernment, too, will be quick and accurate. And, while you instantly separate the wheat from the chaff in your affairs, you'll notice that imperfections no longer hurt or disturb you, as they may have before. The negations and denials of this metaphysical Science (Lesson 2) have the double effect of pointing out the erroneous quickly and rendering any situation immediately harmless.

Whatever we look toward, we become identified with. Gaze often God-ward and you will understand Principle. Gaze often toward our Spirit-Source, Jesus' "Father." and all thoughts shall be like morning music. Lift up the inward vision frequently toward that realm from which Health and Supply derive and experience immediate comprehension of Truth, for "understanding is a wellspring of Life."

I AM

By the study of Spirit we get to know Spirit and realize that the men and women on the streets of restlessness are Spirit; they are, in Truth, walking secrets of the splendor of God. We realize that the trees are in reality Spirit, whispering great secrets of how to be happy and free. We know that all that is real is Mind thinking thoughts that demonstrate goodness and well-being.

Such true thought demonstrates intelligence, and somebody is always wiser when we think a true thought. True thought demonstrates in peace, and somebody is at peace when we think Truth.

Clearly, the power of God is experienced only by means of a true premise, with its irresistible consequences. So we say, "God is all." And, in so saying, we must accept that anything that is not God is nothing — it can't, and doesn't, exist.

So, if *I exist, what must I be? Must I not be God?* And if that part of me that exists, that can say I AM, is God, then that appearance of me which is not Good, or God, is nothing. That which I AM is God. I AM Spiritual Substance; the flesh of this body is appearance, nothing. I AM Truth; I must be the word of Truth or my words are nothing. I AM Mind, and the senses of Mind are seeing, hearing, smelling, tasting, and feeling; so, since God created and saw that it was good, I must see, hear, smell, taste, and feel only Good — all else is nothing.

It is because I am Spirit that I speak the words. I do not say I am Health in order to become healthy, but because I, in my Divine Truth, am Health itself. I tell the Truth about it. I do not say I am owner of the universe in order to get hold of great possessions, but because it's true that as Spirit, I am possessor of all.

We do not take the premise that there are any sick to cure or sinners to reform — as Spirit, our energy demonstrates the nothingness of sickness and sin. We do not think that our brother needs to be cured of swearing or stealing or smoking — we say he is free to do as he pleases, which takes the burden of our heavy supposition off of him and he feels free to cease such activities. To the Holy Spirit all the life and joy and skill of the universe is given, and one need not beg for it nor work for it. It is so; that is all.

- Ω -

THE PRACTICE

Saturday mornings:

Take a premise from this Science and reason with it until the light of understanding breaks over and through you, thrilling your body with that cool fire of recognition.

Breathe in the Spirit of Understanding; with the sixth light of Science we are prepared to meet the world with our own free independence of thought, able to make nothing of its worst appearances.

THE METAPHORS

The Number: SIX

In the Apocrypha[49] we read that in the sixth place the Lord imparts understanding. Six is the number of separation, referring to the apparent separation in the two natures of humanity: the "natural human, or Adam" nature, and the divine or "Christ" nature. Its gift is distinguishing the real from the shadow, this path from that. Six is also the number of complete manifestation, standing for laborless success.

The Stone: Sardius

Sardius ("sardine stone") is also known as ruby, carnelian, chalcedony, or carbuncle. It's the 1st stone in the priest's breastplate as described in Exodus, standing for the tribe of Zebulun, and the 6th wall of the foundation of the New Jerusalem described in

---

[49] *The Apocrypha* are the "hidden" books of the Bible—the books that may be included in the Catholic Bible but not the Protestant, or in the Jewish scriptures but not the Christian, or in the Eastern Orthodox but not the Roman-based churches.

Revelation. It's associated with the "base chakra" or "chi point" in the body. *Zebulun* means "haven," or "dwelling place," and the message is "I am protected." The Sardius stone stands for mystical invocation — the capacity to understand and know things we have not been taught.

The Apostle: Matthew—Clear Sight, the "Gift of the Lord"

The name, Matthew, is the English version of Matthias, which is the Greek version of the Hebrew name, *Mattathjah*, meaning "Gift of Jah, Gift of God." In the New Testament stories, Matthew Levi was a tax collector, hated by the rest of the Jews for having "sold out" to the conquerors by agreeing to collect money from his people, and, of course, keeping a share for himself, which was seen as stealing. This was particularly horrible because he was from the tribe of Levi: those who were descended from the law-givers and destined to be priests. But Matthew met Jesus and was transformed.

Matthew's gospel is considered by some to be the oldest of the New Testament gospels on the assumption that he was probably the only disciple who could write and so the only one who took notes or kept a journal of Jesus' teachings. The Greek version[50] of the story, which is the basis for our New Testament gospel, was probably written about 60-70 c.e. It is, clearly, designed to establish the rationale for Jesus' role as

---

[50] Though traditional scholars believe the Greek documents to be the first written accounts of Jesus' life and teachings, George Lamsa, who spoke Aramaic, went into isolated villages throughout the Middle East and found copies of copies of ancient transcripts, written on parchment in the language Jesus spoke, which he has translated into a new version of the New Testament.

Messiah, emphasizing the links between the Old Testament prophecies and the events in Jesus' life.

Matthew is associated with the heart chakra, which is our link with the divine in the body, and in many cultures is considered the seat of the soul.

His Beatitude is "Blessed are the pure in heart." The Gift of the Lord comes to those who are pure in heart; they can see the reigning principle of Life, even when others do not.

Lesson Seven: Inheritance—The Wellspring of Life

All realizations of Good externalize in good. We train our own realizations first. Then, since the world that emerges around us comes second, we deal with our world secondly. This Science deals with the thoughts, just as Jesus did, and then it speaks of externals. So, in this Science, the first six lessons are devoted to the realization of God in the soul, and the next six are devoted to our relations to the world.

The seventh statement of Moses is, "Let the earth bring forth." Earth here means mind. Let the mind bring forth. What can mind bring forth except thoughts? But Moses is speaking of the Divine Mind, which has not been acknowledged by humanity as the only mind and so has been hidden.

Don't hide it. As you reveal it you are letting it bring forth, for as soon as we uncover the Divine Mind in humanity, it acts by bringing forth fresh life in everybody and everything we meet. It brings out their original health. It strengthens them wonderfully. It brings provisions and bounty to them. It brings them defense and protection from accidents, from trouble, from afflictions.

But all this is only showing more and more of what already exists in Spirit. Remember, even healing is not healing, because Mind needs no healing; Mind being given its freedom is also a statement of appearance only: as God is free, so Mind is free. Moses is using a figure of speech when he says "let Mind (or God, or the earth) do thus and so," for in the Spirit, all is already heavenly, already done. We are to see Spirit. We can see Spirit. And the more of Spirit that we see, the more perfectly we see things.

All things are waiting to be looked upon by us as they really are. If you let the Spirit tell you what is, then there will be no talk about sickness, no discussion of what is distressing anybody. The Soul-Self is the everlasting reality of everyone; the outer body is only the shadow system, hiding the smiling Soul-Self. Whoever turns inward and recognizes continually their own Soul-Self, which is Spirit – Free Omnipotence – must find their outer forms improving in looks, health, strength, and speech.

Likewise, our neighbor has a free, wise, un-killable Soul-Self. Did you ever notice how you feel that the person who realizes your worthiness seems to understand you best? Consider the legendary old Lord Fauntleroy, who had appeared to all people as savage and ugly. His grandson, Little Lord Fauntleroy, could see that his soul was generous and good; he could see nothing else, and praised his grandfather. So the old man would tell people, "Ask Little Lord Fauntleroy. He knows me; he will tell you what I will do." This is true of everybody and everything. They feel that in Truth they are Good, so those who see them as good please them best.

It may seem impossible. You may think that the beastly characters we read about must not be called good. You see very plainly the faults of those you meet every day and think it's impossible for you to call them good. But when we see anything as evil, it signifies how far we are from seeing spiritual Truth. You can see for yourself that if God, or Good, is omnipresent, then that which is not good is not present.

Wherever we find profound thought and feeling — even in the most ancient religions — we find the same thing: nothing exists outside ourselves. In the ancient Hindu text, the Lanka Vetara, we read, "What seems external exists not at all." The Apostle Paul, in his letter to Corinthians, reaffirms this, saying "I am determined not to know anything among you, except the Lord." The realization of God is within ourselves — and we have supreme power over and with our own realizations.

So Moses and Jesus teach the same story: let it be of the Soul that you speak. Let Spirit utter itself. Greed, unkindness, evil disposition are all unreality.

THE POWER OF PRAISE

If I were asked what was the quickest way for a practitioner of this Science to get the healing power going, I would probably say, "Praise everything and everyone in your mind, and speak those praises aloud."

All religions, in one way or another, teach that "As we think, so we are"[51] and "By your words are you justified." The words we speak and the thoughts we think constitute the breath of our mind, as the air constitutes the breath of our body, and there are words that exhilarate the mind, as there are airs that exhilarate the body.

---

[51] James Allen wrote *As A Man Thinketh* in 1902 to show people that this fundamental truth is found across religious traditions. Miller's *As We Think, So We Are* was written to do what this book does: take his Victorian prose and make it approachable by the modern reader.

All inspired writers of fiction describe their character's vision before relating the judgment, and they develop the outward conditions of the people's experience as results that follow from their judgment. Every teacher must bring forth the Responsive Intelligence from within the student, or that teacher has accomplished nothing at all. Across the world, True Science always teaches a practice that results in healing for all its practitioners, and exposes them to All-Peace.

The glory of this metaphysical Science is that, recognizing that our inward visual direction creates our perceptions and expectations, which then translate into material affairs and bodies, its first and fundamental instruction is to exalt the inward vision. It demonstrates that such exalted thoughts may formulate into life-filled bodies and joyous experiences. "He that looks toward me beholds me everywhere."

The Japanese believe that praise of all things exhilarates the mind and then the body, while complaining brings very different results. In 1814 Kurozumi Saki, the young man described earlier as having become a miraculous healer through praise, had become very gloomy by complaining (interestingly, the Japanese term for gloom is *inki*). He had breathed the spirit of gloom until he was actually ill with what was known then as consumption. Finally, he resolved to cease mourning. It was difficult at first, but he began to praise everything and everybody. He went on for some years, breathing into himself an entirely different set of words. He began to be very cheerful, even though his consumption seemed to be getting worse. One night, just as he supposed he was breathing his last, he was praising the rising sun, and a sort of buoyant ecstasy went through him.[52] His breath grew deep and electrifying. He rose from the ground where he had collapsed and found that his breath was the very spirit of cheer, which the Japanese term, *yoki*. His breath was a healing force for others, as well; for years after, if he breathed on deformed or dying people, they were healed.

Praise of the ever-present Provider, the ever-protecting Defender, always meets with response. Praise of the earth's bountiful productivity has caused the earth to teem with plenty. Praise of gold has hurried gold into the coffers of seekers. Praise of beauty has turned heads to seek it above integrity, motherhood, and even spirituality. Praise of labor overruns the world with willing workers seeking employment. "Concerning the work of my hands offer praise and thanksgiving."

The name Judah means "praise of God" or "I sing praise to the Most High." Judah is the tribe of kings among the Hebrews: David, Solomon, and Jesus were all of the tribe of Judah. "The scepter shall not pass from Judah" is the promise of Genesis: the power is in praise.

Recognition is a form of praise. Description is a form of praise. *Even to describe what we do not like magnifies its importance and spreads out its impacts.* "Let none of you imagine evil," said Zechariah, the Old Testament prophet. He gathered all imaginings against ourselves and our fellow beings under one heading and warned humanity to speak only Truth to our neighbor.

No one is so mistaken that we cannot praise their wise, Free Spirit. No one so negligent or reprehensible

---

[52] This is much like the experience Echart Tolle describes in his introduction to *The Power of Now*.

that we cannot praise their integrity and uprightness. No one so old, or sick, or lame that we cannot praise their beautiful, flawless, free divinity.

You may sometimes find yourself seeming to be sick. Though nothing has happened to you, you may appear ill. If so, then you have caught some of the world's false beliefs, or maybe some old notions you used to think are showing themselves. A woman who had been taking on apparent colds whenever a damp draft struck her came upon this Science when in her sixtieth year, and after a while her mental feeling got so strong that drafts never affected her. *No disease comes from material causes,* though the world may speak as if they do. All is in thought first.

There is an elixir in the words of Truth. Keep them going continually: they will change your life and increase your powers. And what is Truth? High praise of the shining wisdom, the divine wholeness of every woman, man, child, animal, tree, plant, stone, and star, throughout all the near and far-stretching expanses, visible and invisible: this is Truth.

THE HEALING MINISTRY

It's possible, by persistent praise of the free Self, to make a total change in someone's appearance. If we're suddenly aware of the free Self that comes sweeping in with our neighbor, a very little silent description of what we sense will cause any gloom of illness or decay to drop away.

We may not yet aware by any inner sense of hearing, seeing, smelling, tasting, or feeling, that the free Soul-Self is present, yet by the reasoning of this metaphysical Science we know it must be present. Then we must go on describing that Soul, praising it and commanding it, that any shadow of pain, sickness, or poverty must move aside for the smile of the Spirit's wellbeing to glow in our neighbor's face and form.

True descriptions are the new Gospel. "Praise the True Self," is the message of the Good news. Do not wail that, though you only seek to know God, little false notions creep into your mind. Do not complain that, though you really love the Highest, your body is not sound. Can't you see that in doing so you're focusing on the errors rather than on "the Lord that heals?" So many clever describers of degraded human conditions are among us! What healing they might be turning their splendid words to, by praising the free, wise, immortal Spirit, instead!

Why would you say that God has afflicted you, if saying such a thing makes you a disease breeder? Why would you say that you feel unhappy, if saying this shuts up a gate against the breath of the spirit of the morning of joy? Don't you choose the thoughts you think? Don't be concerned about any special tendency you may have toward anger or grief or any form of distress. Instead, tell the way of the Spirit so often that she comes stealing through you and you become a health giver and cheer bringer.

Sometimes the way to meet apparent hardships that have clung to us for months or years is not by saying that they are nothing; rather it's by finding the Holy Spirit of them. A young Scientist found herself hoarse and, though other parts of her body quickly healed when told that nothing could ail them, her hoarseness stayed on. One night, after whispering for nearly three months, she said, "You seem to stay around me as if you'd nowhere else to go and belong here, and I have been snubbing you and treating you badly. I will do so no more. As God, with good for me in your presence, I bid you welcome in love. You may stay with me as long as you please." In the morning she was cured. She realized that a sense of gloom had left her as well — she'd touched on the same principle as the Japanese healer Saki had, decades before: she had replaced gloom and illness with praise and appreciation

OVERCOMING FEAR

Much material misfortune can be traced to dread or fear of people's influence or opposition. Jesus said to agree with your adversary quickly. He meant to take up that person that you've dreaded and establish that you're not afraid of them, that they must be Good as you are Good.[53]

Be clear that no one can enter the sphere of life where you dwell except as pure Good. Your thoughts thus push any seeming evil away and leave the Holy Spirit, the Soul-Self of your neighbor, free to do you great good. You may lead your own free life and, though there may at first seem to be real hurts caused by them, as the mind grows stronger you forget all feelings of dread and repugnance toward anyone, and drop even the memory of the things that brought it on.[54]

---

[53] Emilie Cady, in *Lessons in Truth*, tells us that the individuality of God in each of us is always stronger than the personality of another being, and that God is the individuality of everyone.

[54] *A Course in Miracles* says, "You know you've forgiven someone when all you remember is the love between you."

If through fear, you don't speak audibly about things, you must redouble your thoughts and speak them a few times to your seeming discredit. If you are timid about telling people that they are well NOW, I would advise you to run the risk of your pride a few times. Say, like the Denver doctor, "I don't care if you appear to be sick, I don't believe in sickness and I think this is all imagination. You must be sitting up by the end of the hour and well by tomorrow."

You may fear that it won't come out right and people will think you are foolish, and tell others so. Can't you put your reputation in the hands of Omnipotent Truth? Which do you suppose had the larger practice: the cheerful, buoyant doctor who always told his patients that they would get well, or those who tried to be "sensible" and judge by appearances? Of course it was the cheerful one! His presence was a tonic for the families, and their cheerful feelings buoyed up the sick ones' minds and revitalized them. By contrast, the reasoning out of a patient's apparent malady like an intellectual problem too often leads the patient to catch fear, instead of healing.

Perfect love of your Science takes away your fear, and *after a while you don't talk the Science much. Instead, you heal by some hearty, simple, cheerful word that bubbles over from your constant thoughts of health and life*, irresistible spiritual vigor, and unhidden goodness in everyone. You will be like the doctor who is said to have laughed his patients well, who found everything they did and said so uproarious that his patients would get to laughing in spite of themselves. He would sit and fiddle with some remedy or other, telling the patient that he was more scared than hurt, that he was resting up a bit and would be all right soon[55]. Many a seemingly dying patient was laughed back to life in this way—the grooves of their minds were changed.

Another doctor went to see an old schoolmate and found her seemingly breathing her last. Reminiscing with her he asked, in his boyish tone of voice, "Do you remember the crow's nest?" He said a little more, not to urge or coax her to think back to those days, but simply sharing a fond memory. It brought back to her mind the faint memories of her happy girlhood, with its liveliness and strength. That change of mind cured her.

A great healer once said that he always kept his mind dwelling on the enchanting airs of summertime. He remembered how the chirp of grasshoppers and the far away song of birds and brooks sounded. Then he would feel the soft flakes of health drop down into his mind and float into and through his flesh—like snowflakes gently absorbed by his skin.

You won't be afraid to tell patients how the snowflakes of healing are falling around them all the time if your heart is sure of it, but you'll be wise enough not to speak of such seeming impossibilities if your heart is full of certainty, for you'll see that your presence is all the speech they need.

GUIDELINES FOR TREATMENT

Learn to get exactly right ideas and you will, after a while, educate the world by just thinking this Science. You don't have to tell someone they don't have a

---

[55] Although this story was told over a hundred years ago, a modern physician, the clownish Patch Adams, has discovered the same method and applied it with great success all over the world.

disease, that they never took a chill, or whatever, if every bit of them is convinced that they "caught the flu." You treat them silently. You need not talk all the time about any point in Science, but simply know the Truth.

There was a young metaphysical practitioner[56] who had spoken mighty praises one morning of the way that God, as the health and salvation of the people, would work through her to will and to do. She had been troubled by her apparent lack of success as a healer, but she meekly acknowledged that God was doing great things for her, through her, and by her, whether she had seen so or not. Her first case that morning was a lame man, and though she felt great compassion for him, she had no thoughts, for she felt that if God didn't manifest through her there was no way she could make anything happen. This sense held her silent, almost helpless, as if she were nothing at all and God were all.

All at once, without realizing she was going to, she told the man to throw down his crutch and try to walk across the room. He obeyed willingly and found he could limp without his crutch very well. She had him try two or three times more and he was cured. It seemed as if his flesh and muscles had drunk the elixir of this new mental atmosphere. The little woman, unsure of herself, had made herself so silent that the voice of the Spirit could speak to the waiting soul of the man.

We all are free within our own Spirit. This is a Truth that everyone who has gotten into the habit of unconsciously yielding to the collective belief of one kind or

---

[56] In all likelihood, this is a story about Emma, herself, spoken in the third person as was typical of the period.

another is eager to receive. Once a practitioner[57] had a woman come asking to be cured of catarrh. Putting down her head, the practitioner silently let the Spirit speak through her. Then she waited a moment and to the woman she silently said, "I pronounce you free from the thoughts of other people. You think your own noble thoughts. You are free, whole, cleansed, and good. You are healed! In the name of the Father and of the Son and of the Holy Spirit I pronounce you well and strong and at peace through and through." The woman was instantly freed of all appearance of symptoms.

You will have the same kind of results for similar situations. The patient whose condition is a result of accepting common belief will be immediately healed.

If you don't see immediate relief, repeat the same treatment. And if not then, give the same treatment again. Three times are not too many to give one message.

There's been no practitioner of the Science who has struck the spring with such perfect understanding that he worked out his cures with perfect constancy. There are moments when your healing power will be wonderful. When those moments are gone, you may feel mournful, but you must not mourn even about that, for your power lays in praise: you are to be cheerful under all circumstances as cheer is a praise-full feeling. The cheerfulness may even rise to ecstasy, at which point, the healing is instantaneous.

You need not worry about whether you should speak. If you have taken the fresh morning for giving thanks and glad praises to the Spirit, speaking forth

---

[57] Again, probably describing Emma's own experience.

freely some lesson of this Science, your mind and aura will be filled with all the blessed qualities of God through the day. You are a miracle-worker by inherent right. Give your free Soul the chance to do all your thinking and all your speaking.

If the patient were to return another day with the same complaint, you must change your treatment, but I'll talk about that in the next lesson.

Remember. *There is in reality no disease or imperfection whatever.* When you realize this strongly, I hope you won't treat anyone, for this realization is in itself a treatment.

ALL METHODS THE SAME

Truth takes away all our dependence upon outside help—or even what may seem to be outside help. We learn to see God in the apparently sick person as Health, because we know that as Health, God is there. We learn to see strength in the apparently feeble old woman, because God as Strength is there. You may breathe Strength itself by talking to Strength itself. If you praise the Holy Spirit for this strength, you'll be surprised how it will take hold of you. There's an uplifting aura around one who knows he is strong in Spirit. Our Strength rises and goes forward to all, because we know that It is God; It goes forth just by our knowing that it is so.

So there's really no need to study the past—even the symbols and teachings of Moses and Jesus. In this metaphysical Science we realize this knowledge without going back to pick men's thoughts. But we are human and inclined to look through the old files of thought that made people miracle-workers. Moses worked miracles; what idea did he hold that made him able to? We find the mind of the man in his writings. A miracle-worker speaks; what did she say?

Yet, though we wish to hear, the power was not the words; it was God. God with them, in them, through them, is the same God from whom we seek to receive the same healing knowledge. That is the secret of healing. The method and words are nothing.

Faith is the curative principle; the words are nothing. And faith, as we learned in Lesson Four, is a mind fixed firmly on the Good. All the words about health just express the practitioner's feeling as nearly as possible. The more perfectly the practitioners' words express what they are feeling, though they may be only thinking silently, the more real the health of the patient becomes in their experience. *The words are simply the vehicles of the practitioner's feelings that go out and touch the apparently ailing.*

The more spiritually intense the feeling that the practitioner has, the more certain the cure is to be permanent. Yet it isn't the feelings that heal; people have often felt strongly that their patients are cured when they have still seemed to ail.

Whatever method is used, it is the same. The Japanese youth breathed upon his patients. The German priest made the sign of the cross and cried with a loud voice, "In the name of the Father and of the Son and of the Holy Ghost, let the disease be gone!" In Zoroastrianism, the oldest of western religions, "one may heal by herbs, another by the will, but it is by the divine word that the sick are most surely healed." But it is no more the words that heal than it is the herbs. We all know that one person may use the words faithfully and not cure the case, while another may use the same words and heal the case in a few minutes. In our time we find people being healed by many different means, though those who rely on material methods are apt to forget that all healing is God's Presence at work. Still, whenever they begin to acknowledge that God is the health of the people, you'll find them using fewer and fewer material means.

Some practitioners, faced with patients who have forgotten the Cause of well-being, have thought out great reasonings about God as a healing presence and have shown forth good health and invigorated lives. Reasoning about the presence of God and telling about the character of God often makes the cure affect other needs of the patients besides bodily disease, as well; they are often turned away from their old habits, or even change their tastes.

How shall we absolutely understand how to heal the sick? Paul said it is by letting "the same Mind be in you that was in Christ Jesus." Moses said the same in his own symbolic fashion.

Now the Christ Mind "thinketh no evil, is not puffed up, is not angry, is not vain, is not critical, is full of praise."[58] And so must we. I will call to your attention the fact that after a short time, vain or critical or proud thoughts seem to stop the healing power of those who, at one time, were quite strong workers. The vain mind does not feel praise-full toward others, and constant praise is what has made so many healers successful.

---

[58] This is from Paul's first letter to the Corinthians in the New Testament, in which he is describing the qualities of Love. Love is another name for the Good that is God.

"Choose this day whom ye will serve... for two shall be in the field; one will be taken, the other left," said Jesus, for all description, silent or audible, brings its outward exhibition. Choosing the downward direction means descriptions—and the experience—of lust and loneliness, death and defeat, disease and dementia. Choosing the High Truth beyond ordinary perception means constant praise for ever-present Good, the Saving Grace that heals and provides in all times and places. The exhibition of our choice will happen speedily, if the inner conviction is alive, and more slowly if the inward conviction has not yet been enlivened by the energy of constant attention.

Healings are works of Truth brought about by faith. As your faith is more firmly established in Truth, you'll find more and more people around you to be well, or easily recovering from maladies, through their association with you, while you do nothing but focus on these twelve propositions of metaphysical Science.

So we make a practice of praising everybody and everything, and above all expressing daily appreciation for all that God works through Spirit. As you continue to do so, you'll find that those who come to you are easily healed. Soon, your patients will be healed before they arrive; then you will never see any sick people. And the secret of healing is, more and more, becoming the inheritance of the world.

- Ω -

THE PRACTICE.

Monday Afternoons:

Clear your own thoughts, saying the following until it feels real to you:

> I, as Spirit, do not accuse the world or myself of lust, greed, or attachment to material objects; all that I see and experience, everywhere I look, is good.

With a Client:

Speak the name of the person, then speak it again, feeling the connection between you.

Now speak the following words with feeling, allowing the Truth of them to flow into and through you to the one you're thinking of — until the Presence within begins to speak for you:

> You are Spirit, therefore you are not afflicted with any kind of disease or distress. I see you in Spirit, as the Health that you are. The Spirit knows nothing of imperfection. The Spirit shines through all your being with its clear, holy light.
>
> From first to last, in your real life, no error has fastened upon you, therefore there is no disease or imperfection in you. Nothing can spoil Universal Health.
>
> You were not born of flesh, according to the law of flesh, but of Spirit, according to the law of Spirit.
>
> Any apparent lust, greed, and attachment to material objects of the generations before you cannot have descended upon you in disease. God, the Good that is in everything, is your Father and Mother. You cannot have inherited disease.
>
> The collective belief has not touched you with thoughts of lust, greed, or attachment, therefore disease does not touch you. God, the Good, enfolds you completely.

People with whom you are associated do not burden you with their thoughts and beliefs of the senses. You are not subject to the thoughts or feelings of others, therefore you cannot have disease in your mind.

Your own thoughts of things of matter, or about attachments or appetites, have no power in them to give you disease. You are in the Spirit, free from your own passions and appetites, therefore you are cleansed by spiritual thoughts now and are well.

My own thoughts and beliefs do not burden you. You are free of any error that appears in me. You are free in the Spirit.

You are free from all thoughts of disease. God, your Good, is your life. You cannot be threatened with death of any part of your life, nor can you fear death, nor yield to death of any part of your life, forever.

God is your health, omnipresent. You cannot be threatened with disease in any part of your health, nor fear disease, nor yield to disease in any part of your body forever.

God is your strength, omnipotent. You cannot be threatened with weakness, nor fear weakness, nor yield to weakness in your strength forever.

God is your substance, the essence of your being, therefore health is God in every part of your body.

You are clearly, and wholly, Spirit; I see you as Wisdom, looking toward me to speak of your heavenly wholeness and peace. I see you as Peace, facing me as Peace that the world cannot take away. I see the child of God that you are: well, whole, wise, and peace-full. Here, now, and always.

In this moment, you are ready to acknowledge to all and to yourself that you are healed. You are in harmony with your life in every way.

And I now realize that you ARE healed! I praise you for your life in the Spirit! I praise you for your strength in the Spirit! I praise you for your perfect manifestation of God NOW! For as God is, you are, always and everywhere. Amen.

[These words are suggestions, only; feel free to use whatever similar words are inspired within you.]

As you feel called to, give this treatment for this person twice more during the week. Continue each Monday afternoon and through the week until it's clear to you and others that the shadow-self has drifted away to reveal the True, Free Soul-Self of the person.

Daily:

Take an hour each morning for some special message for yourself. Have an hour in the afternoon for some words of Truth to the world.

Through the day, practice speaking and thinking only praise-full thoughts toward your Free Self and that of your neighbor. Every time you see your neighbor outwardly as sick or poor or unhappy, remember the Real Self.

Remember that "where two or more are gathered," the Presence is always felt. Be open to the possibility of a comrade, or partner, in your praise and work,[59] someone to face you with your own Divine Self when you may have forgotten.

THE METAPHORS.

The Number: SEVEN.

Seven is the holy number: the number of wholeness. Seven days in a week, seven candles in a standard menorah, seven sins, seven virtues, seven pillars of

---

[59] Many of Emma's students made it a practice to always work in twos: one to treat the client and one to treat the practitioner.

wisdom (a name for the stars in the constellation Pleiades). Seven is the number of creation—seven days and nights. Seven is the power of speech: God speaks the creation; The Book of Revelation says when the 7th angel begins the repetition of the 7th praise, "the mystery of God shall be finished." "And when he had opened the 7th seal, there was silence in Heaven..." — heaven is harmony and perfect speech leads to peace and harmony. "In the seventh place the Lord imparted them speech, an interpreter of the cognitions," says Ecclesiastes. Enoch, "the seventh from Adam," is described in Genesis as a perfected human. Seven is, ultimately, the expansion of power into form.

The Stone: Chrysolite.

Strength of character and purity of vision are the qualities of this golden clear, light-reflecting stone. The word chrysolite means "touch of gold." Compressed to extreme hardness and durability by the weight of ages in the heart of the Earth, it has been transformed from leafy mud into pure light-reflecting beauty, a form of diamond. It signifies right communication: words and thoughts that are well-being. Chrysolite covers the seventh wall of the New Jerusalem and is the fifth stone in the Hebrew priest's breastplate, standing for the tribe of Joseph, the son of Israel who was sold into Egypt by his brothers, interpreted Pharoah's dream, and became the chief steward of the land.

The Apostle: Bartholomew, Imagination.

Bartholomew is the Greek version of the Hebrew name *Bar Tolmai*, meaning "son of Tolmai" or "son of the plowed or furrowed." He is called Nathanael in the gospel of John, so some scholars believe that the full name of this disciple was *N'thanael bar Tolmai*, or "God's Giving, the son of the furrowing." He is associated with the chakra, or energy center, located at the genitals, a source of creativity. According to the Gospels, he was seen by Jesus through "remote viewing" ("e.s.p.") before they met.

The peaceable nature of Nathanael Bartholomew is the true nature of all beings, for Peace is omnipresent. To rebuke someone for their apparent behavior is to be blind to the Truth of that person, their Christ nature. So when another seems to rebuke us, we forgive ourselves and them, we judge not nor accept the judgment of others, and so become peacemakers.

Bartholomew's beatitude is, not too surprisingly, "Blessed are the peacemakers."

Lesson Eight: Truth—Rending the Veil

The eighth lesson in metaphysical Science is "Be not deceived." These are the words of Jesus. Spirit never deceives. Matter is the only deceiver; it makes up all appearances, being formulated by thoughts concerning a kind of God who never existed.

Job's friends described one kind of God, but Job knew another. Their kind of God was full of punishment for exactly the sort of character they described Job to be. Job insisted he was not that character and they must have imagined what they were saying. He permitted himself to experience only the Presence of the infinitely loving Creative Source, and so Job was restored.

Thus it is with all of us. *We look at others in the red or green or blue tints of our own ideas and we see them as entirely different from what they are in reality.* So, what we describe as their character since it's not the truth about them, must be in our own mind in some way. Then, when we get the punishments that we believe should be theirs, we are utterly astonished and grieved, and feel ourselves much abused.

This is why the righteous are strangely afflicted. Too often they, more than any other class of people, see faults in their fellowmen. Ezekiel wanted proper punishments to be meted out for sins. So did the Zoroastrians, and they experienced pestilence, drought, and famine as a result of perceiving wickedness around them.

So, "be not deceived," about either human beings or God, for *all humanity and God, in truth, are Good*. In the Hindu sacred text, the *Bhagavad Gita*, Krishna, as the Spirit of God, says, "Whoever, undeluded, knows me as the Supreme Spirit, worships me in all forms." Such a person, "letting forms remain, opposing nothing, but nowise deceived, recognizes Me in all people and in all things." In other words. such a one knows and feels completely that Spirit is the only substance.

This means that each of us is Spirit. If all being is Spirit, then I am Spirit. And *if Spirit cannot be in poverty or debt, I cannot be in poverty or debt. If Spirit cannot be burdened, I cannot be burdened. If Spirit cannot be sick, I cannot be sick*. All these conditions are nothing to Spirit and so are nothing to me — I am not deceived by any of them, in my own life or in that of those around me.

This is the only understanding that works practically, bringing external forms into new combinations. *We worship Spirit, appreciating the gifts of Spirit, in all its forms — and we let the forms alone*. We don't try to change them; they change themselves by our recognition of Spirit.

We have no inclination to condemn others for not doing what we see as a need. If we were to hate tobacco, or hate rum, or hate any man or woman, we would put up a dark screen between ourselves and the sight of good health in the patient we're trying to cure. If someone has a mournful disposition, it's because they believe the Divine has disappointed them in some way, and this position is like a blot on their ability to see health in a patient — or themselves.

If I thought that doctors of medicine were in great error because they think that drugs and procedures are necessary for healing, I'd be stopping some energy of the Spirit from flowing freely through me. *I need to remember that whether someone thinks healing occurs through drugs or through words, the healing power is moving through whoever has confidence that Omnipotent Good is Omnipresent Health.* Truth that is God, the Good, must, by universal law, stand in the place of appearances, and as we learn Truth, we are masters of the law.

As you see that Truth can't be imaginings or appearances, you come to realize that *you don't have to make your Truth work. You simply know it.* You know the Truth that makes you free. You speak it, and it is its own working principle.

Don't be deceived by your imaginations. Live by Principle, instead. As we reason by Principle, we soon learn to know the meaning of all things; we know exactly what to do. So, let reasoning based on a good solid principle guide your life, and as imaginations arise, let them alone. The simple knowledge that they are imaginings will render them null and void.

LIGHTS IN THE FIRMAMENT

This eighth lesson is about light. It's about freedom. On the material plane, light is the freest process of nature. You cannot bottle it up and if you hide a flame under a bushel, it burns the bushel and makes an even greater light! You may hide it behind some screen, but you cannot quench it by confining it. The doctrine of metaphysical Science is an unquenchable light, and, as you go over the lessons, sometime along the way, you will catch the fire of the Holy Spirit and begin to live the doctrine. "The righteous shall shine like the sea."

Humanity yearns for a country and comradeship that cannot be found except by looking toward the eternal, enduring Universe — the reality of which our material world is but a shadow. For there is eternal light, eternal peace, eternal love, and it is here and now, wherever we are, forever wooing us to look toward it that we may find ourselves and our environments blessed with its everlasting newness.

Moses said, "Let there be lights in the firmament." The soft, starlit night is a symbol for the rest that the mind takes at certain stages along the way, as is the Sabbath: time when we speak nothing, think nothing, do nothing. We have spoken Truth and it does its own work.

And the Truth is that Good is at hand. "The kingdom of heaven is within you," said Jesus. The Brahmin priests of India said, "Around this visible nature there exists another, unseen and eternal, which, when all created things perish, does not perish." The ancient Egyptians spoke of "the Perfect Land" beyond this world of the senses. Hebrew rabbis, studying the *Kabbalah*, describe "the Archetypal world, the *Yesod*, the nourishment of all the worlds."[60]

Therefore, leaving the shows of human misery, and often rejecting them, we "seek the Lord and His strength" and glance upward often toward the Truth that is our salvation, instead. "By persistent attention toward the Divinity Self, the ageless Son of God," The

---

[60] These are more examples of the "monistic idealism" or "Neoplatonism" that philosophers call this way of thinking.an ideal version exists, of which we perceive an imperfect reflection in our normal way of thinking.

great Greek philosopher Plato found that "nothing can injure the immortal principle of the soul."

Keep the eye single to One, Free, Self-existent God and you can't help but believe in Free Grace. Persistence of vision is a scientific term. It was called one-pointedness by the Hindu Brahmins, and the ancient Persian Zoroastrians taught that wherever the eye of divinity is focused, all other senses follow. As Peter did, standing upon the water, we keep our eye on our Lord, because we, too, when we cast our eye downward, will sink.

The ancient Parsees of India[61] discovered that watching things that spoil and die affected them with spoiling matter, but frequent uplifting of the inward vision freed them of such spoiling.[62] Similarly, the vision of a suffering Jesus on the cross only brings more pain and suffering into one's life – slowly but certainly, as those who've shown signs of the stigmata have proved: St. Francis of Assisi focused for years on the pain of Jesus and ultimately experienced the same five wounds in his own body. Padre Pio, a 20th century Italian, did likewise.

But our vision of the risen, Christ-empowered Jesus, with its glorious, healing light, works quickly, indeed. So it's high time we set our inner gaze upon that

---

[61] The Parsees are a group of Persians who migrated to India about a thousand years ago, bringing their traditional Zoroastrian religion with them. They are the ones who build the Taj Majal.
[62] The Japanese researcher Masura Emoto known for his experiments with water crystals, describes experiments in which rice has been placed in two jars, one with a label saying words like, "thank you; we love you," and the other saying things like, "you fool; I hate you," and people spoke similar words to the jars each day for a month. At the end, the rice that was thanked had fermented into a pleasant malted grain and the other had rotted.

holy light, "He who heals all our diseases, who redeems our life from destruction, who crowns us with loving kindness and tender mercy," who said, "Seek ye my face and live."

The ancient Chaldeans called it the Stately Soul; the Brahmins, the Real Self of our self; the Hebrews, the Angel of God's Presence; and Christians call it the ever-present Christ, the Comforting Holy Spirit who said "Nothing shall by any means hurt you ... I am with you always."

When we love and persist in the reasonings we have worked out by this metaphysical Science, we are in full light. Then we are "seeking the kingdom first" and "all else follows."

When we listen to the opinions of others, or side with our imaginations, we plunge into darkness at once. Then our intellect must be the stars in our night sky. And if, in our intellect, we believe that God, our Good, is far away, then the stars will seem far away and the night seem dark and cold.

The reasonings of metaphysical Science are the works of Spirit. They are the works of Truth. Truth is in us: let it shine. Eternal reasoning[63] is eternal day, so let reasoning based on Truth be your light. Truth performs great tasks: let it shine as miracles of well-being, cheering and enlightening the nations.

---

[63] "Reason" is the name that Ralph Waldo Emerson gave to the knowing that comes from deep within when all normal thought has stopped. "Reasoning," as used by Emma, is the process of working out in thought a line of logic that takes one to that deep knowing where no normal thought is possible. Both approaches could also be called "contemplative prayer."

SIGNS OF THE SPIRIT

In ancient times, the sign of the cross was made as a sign of erasure. The cross is the sign of undoing the past by seeing and hearing the New, from heaven to earth (up to down) and across the land (left to right). The ancient Egyptians and Chaldeans (where Abraham came from) made the sign of the cross to signify that the present state of affairs is blotted out. The Etruscan high priests who lived in Italy before the Greeks came, stood on the highest hill of what is now Rome and, moving their and from above their head to below their waste, and then across their chest, were saying "All is well; from Heaven to Earth and from Sea to Sea." When Greeks and Romans wet the finger with spittle to make the sign, they were signifying that what was presenting itself was nothing at all: the unseen Spirit was all.

Jesus called his miracles, or works of Truth, signs. He said that they tell us where someone stands in his spiritual life. Working to make something happen is evidence of a mind focusing on material things, for *when we are spiritual we need not try to bring great things to pass — they simply come to pass as the outworking of Truth.*

Those who think Truth will be immaculately neat in dress and person, but it will be the natural, unpremeditated movement of that immaculate Spirit that is the focus of their thoughts. They'll be very honorable in their dealings with others, but it will not be because they're thinking about their duties — rather the duties are performed because they are thinking about the principles of Truth.

As we live in the light of this reasoning, or Spirit, we see our words attending to our external circumstances, so we let go of any concern over them, obeying both Jesus and Krishna by taking no thought for what we eat, drink, or wear. While the apostle Paul often focused on material things—at one moment it was meat, and another it was the length of a man's or woman's hair—these subjects are not even in the mind of someone who is Spirit-focused. Rather, they show a conflicted intellect.

By contrast, as we contemplate Truth, the words we speak are the utterance of the Spirit of Life within us. They point to the Spirit and go forth from the Spirit and the works of Spirit shine as signs of the Light that we all are. So we speak certain words after we become spiritual, and when this has been observed by others, they've insisted that speaking those words made us spiritual, seeing the effect as a cause, and have set rules requiring people to speak only that way.

Some who become spiritually minded lose their taste for certain foods. Seeing this, religious leaders have proclaimed that everyone should abstain from those foods—again mistaking the effect for a cause. Fasting from food has never made people spiritual, for material actions are not the cause of Spirit. The reverse is the way of the law: *according to the Spirit in us, so will our outer actions be.*

FORMS ARE NOTHING; LIGHT IS ALL.

It's the goal of this eighth lesson to convince humanity to erase all fictitious estimates of the reality around us. To love is to see God in all. This light, this love, puts out any appearance of evil—as a lamp dispels darkness. *Any other sight than pure beauty — any sight of lack, scar, or deformity — is imagination.*

So also with intelligence: even the greatest minds tell how limited they feel their own knowledge to be, and how incompetent they sometimes feel. But that's not how people who are in the light of reasoning feel, being based upon the principle that God is Wisdom, omnipresent. The Understanding Absolute is *in* them, informing them of high Truth. So, to speak of ignorance is to speak of imaginings: as you are Spirit, so must you be Intelligence and Wisdom, for such is Spirit.

Remember, there is One above thought, above intellect. The rabbis studying the Kabbalah call it the *Ain Soph*. The Brahmins of India reject outer sounds and inner memories of sorrows and human vexations until they are left alone with it, calling it *Brahman*, the Universal Consciousness. "Take no thought," said Jesus, but "look up."

How can the ears hear the Truth regarding an apparently blind person, when the blindness seems real and sad? Only the words of the Healing Spirit have life and strength.

GUIDELINES FOR TREATMENT

"Relax your body," say certain practitioners among us. "Drop sights and sounds, drop emotions; cease your thoughts and become blank for a few moments." This is their way of letting go, of rejecting old thoughts. "Allow one positive thought to fill your mind," they say. "Hold the thought firmly. It will, in time, demonstrate in outward conditions." This is their way of replacing the old thought with a new one.

A young man was treating a lady against coughing. He was very eager to help her, and told her a great many reasons why her cough was not real, but all the time her cough troubled him. She kept on coughing for six weeks, to his great dismay. Finally, he said the cough was nothing to him, that she might cough all she liked. From that day she never coughed again.

The young practitioner had hit on the implication in this eighth lesson: *"Leave forms alone; they are nothing to us."* Such an attitude toward the world of matter is the quickest way to get rid of anything appearing to be abnormal, diseased, or ugly—which would feed and grow on our feeling badly about them, or talking and thinking about them as something that disturbs us. Notice that the cough was not cured until he gave up thinking it was his burden to cure her. He let the Spirit tell the Truth about it, then both he and the woman were free.

Spirit never mourns over robberies nor deaths, nor over pain and crying. They are nothing to Spirit, and those who suddenly realize that *any sort or kind of evil is nothing at all*, have touched on the second treatment of outer conditions. This feeling comes by denying the seeming and affirming the real. It opens the eyes to see purely from a spiritual standpoint; that which sees evil is no intelligence at all.

So deny the inheritance of sin. Deny the personal sin. Deny humanity's inequities. Fear nothing from the suggestion of evil. Deny that you have ever wronged anyone, for in you—and every being—is God only.

Whether in business, politics, or sickness, don't imagine that there are any lustful passions or attachments lurking behind appearances, or that good appearances are hiding evil conditions. And do not consider there to be anything wrong with a business that seems successful and flourishing. All that looks well is making a heroic attempt to be God's good way in your eyes. Believe in it. Speak kindly of it.

If your patient comes to you a second time with any appearance of malady, or if your affairs do not correct themselves after a treatment, it's a sign that you've accepted statements of evil against somebody or something, imagining that while they may not seem bad they're hiding badness.

This is deception. If anybody or anything appears good it is our pleasure to believe it is genuine goodness.

Do not allow yourself to believe that any man or woman, child, or object, hides evil though it appears good. If you do, your client will not return saying in joyful affirmation, "I am totally cured!" because you would have been deceived, rather than filled with the light of Truth.

- Ω -

THE PRACTICE.

Tuesday Afternoons:

Take Tuesday afternoons to blot out all the words of sickness, pain, and death that may appear in your environment. Take Tuesday to erase the pain, poverty, and disease from over the free Spirit in those around you. Then speak the words:

> Around me and before me, in the plain sight of my body and in my soul, all is perfect power, ready to rise to accomplish the works of God, the Good.
>
> The words that I speak, I speak not of myself, but the All-sustaining Source that dwells within me, Infinite

Power does them. God, my Good, works through me to will and to do that which is my fulfillment. Amen.

With a Returning Case:

Take Tuesday to hearken to the particular message that belongs to Monday's case, then call to mind the name of the person and, feeling the connection between you, say:

I am not deceived into believing in you as diseased.

You have not inherited the formulations of deception; you have inherited only Truth.

You have not been deceived by the collective consciousness formulating deceptions around you; you are surrounded by God.

You have not been deceived by the people around you; there is no gathering of sin nor is there any possibility of consequences of sin; you are free.

You do not hear sin, see sin, feel sin, fear sin, from anywhere; you are free in purity.

You have not formulated self-deceptions; nor have you formulated any deception between you and me; there is no cause for disease or distress in Spirit.

I do not believe in the formulations of deception by any means, whatever. I believe only in the clean handwriting of God on every part of your mind, and standing forth from every part of your body.

You are now showing forth perfection through every manifestation of your being. You have heard the Truth of God. You express the Truth of God. I see through you, in you, and by you, perfect well-being, throughout. You are every whit whole.

You are therefore ready, now, to acknowledge that your life is perfect. You acknowledge this truth to all around you, to yourself, and to me, now.

In the name of the Father/Mother Almighty, the Miracle-working Heir, and the Holy Breath of Spirit Present,

I pronounce you healed and whole, manifesting perfect well-being in all aspects of your life, now and forever. Amen.

[These words are suggestions, only; feel free to use whatever similar words are inspired within you.]

Daily:

It will be good to write out your treatments and their results. And if new ideas come to you, put them down. Many a case of apparent sickness would come out for more enduring health if we would write out our treatments and read them over and over by ourselves. And many healings would be recognized and remembered if they had been recorded.

THE METAPHORS.

The Number: EIGHT

Eight is the number of awakened awareness. An infant is circumcised on the 8th day, symbolizing being cut off from stories of pain, disease, poverty, and death, and listen intently to the heavenly speech. The risen Jesus came into visible presence after eight days. Peter, James, and John heard Moses and Elijah with Jesus after eight days on the mountain. Aeneas kept to his bed for eight years, waiting for the right word, which Peter spoke to him. With eight, true genius and strength have evolved.

The Stone: Beryl

Beryl is the foundation stone for the eighth wall of the New Jerusalem, the emerging "place of peace." It's the color of both land and sea, and stands for the written record. Those who have touched the beryl stone are those who hear the word of healing—and their written words convey health to all who read them.

The Apostle: Philip, Love.

Philip is said to have spoken Greek so well that he has no recorded Hebrew name and was sometimes referred to as "the Greek." His name, Philip, is Greek and means "lover of horses." The horse is a symbol for the power, swiftness and strength of a principle. The love is born of knowledge and understanding of what is being focused on. As the mother knows the son is good, regardless of what others may say, and in time is proven out, so with the love of Philip.

Philip is said to have asked "can anything good come out of Nazareth?" prior to meeting Jesus, and to have seen immediately that the Master metaphysician was the embodiment of Good.

If a principle is clear to you and easily understood, stand by it and focus on it, swiftness and strength are in its legs. If you love someone, seeing the Truth of their being unswervingly and negating the possibility of any other behaviors, you can trust that any tangles between you will be straightened out in time, no matter what people around you may say. Philip is associated with the root chakra, the source of power.

The Beatitude is, "Blessed are those who are persecuted for the sake of their righteousness, for theirs is the kingdom of heaven." The early Christian martyrs who saw only Good are said to have experienced lions and spears as angels and flowers coming to carry them to a new place of peace.

Lesson Nine: Holiness—Right Discernment

Moses said, "The sins of the fathers shall be visited upon the children until the 3rd and 4th generation." As a result, too often, innocent children are supposed to be under the curse of their father's or mother's evil thoughts and character and too many have lain down under the burden of deathly illness because it seemed too heavy to carry. Too many others have fallen under the burden of kleptomania, intemperance, or depression because they believed their parents left these things as their inheritance.

But what kind of a god would visit his own people with such a law as that? Not Jesus' Abba. "Neither hath this man sinned nor his parents," he told questioners about the man blind from birth.

Did Jesus believe in sin? "Go and sin no more," was the most he had to say about any sinful nature. So who has sinned and is affected by sin? Only the illusory person, the Adam being. Jesus let the Spirit free, putting away all identification with matter and the flesh. "No man is your Father upon the earth," he told his disciples, "Call no man your father."

This ninth lesson calls our attention to the Undifferentiated, Ever-facing Original, which the Egyptians called Soul, the Persian Magi called Self, the Hebrews called God or the Angel of the Presence, and which is, in truth, Spirit. This lesson brings to our speech the I AM that glows with unquenchable might at the center of every living being. So we sing with the great mystic and writer, Victor Hugo, saying, "The Highest God and the Inmost God is one God."

NO ACCUSATION

Recognition of the Divine must come from the God-center of our being. At this magnetic Center, we are "the Sun of righteousness... with healing in its wings." No accusation abides at that Center; it is pure love, asking nothing in return. No condemnation abides with the awakened Joy spark, "I came not to condemn," said Jesus.

Accusations come from mistaken ideas called prejudices; they do not emanate from the one Mind. Prejudice against a religion acts against one's business judgment as well as health. Prejudice against people will very likely hit one's business affairs. Prejudice against alcohol, tobacco, or other drugs is equally limiting.

The thoughtful person has always linked holiness and health, sin and disease. Both health of the body and health of one's business affairs have been understood as the result of righteous action. Too often, however, the opposite has been assumed—that distress is the result of mistaken action.

Plato taught that the whole world is a colossal system of shadows. The Buddhists and Hindus teach similarly, speaking of all as maya, which has been translated as illusion, but means something more like the projections on a movie screen. It's said that elephants sometimes fight shadows on the rocks until they have beaten themselves into pieces. Similarly, missionaries and activists, fighting the great shadow of belief in somebody doing great wrongs in the world, burn out with the feeling of how gigantic the monsters are who have this poor world in their jaws. They have been deceived: *the deepest shadow is belief in wrong-doing.* Its shadows appear as long stretches of hardship over your pathway, which in Truth is all light with the glory of Goodness.

How much of the ineffectiveness of humanity comes from thinking about wrong-doings — of our own or of others! Effectiveness comes with letting the goodness of the merciful and tender Spirit speak, instead of your condemning tendencies, wherever anything appears to be evil. So make sin and ignorance as unreal to your mind as matter and evil.

If you feel as though you ought to be protecting yourself from others, physically, financially or as to your reputation, stop and think over this lesson. You must not put up umbrellas against things which don't exist. By this I mean, if God is your world, what is there to fear?

In this world, each of us has all we can do to look to the ways of our own heart, ensuring that our thoughts and world are in harmony by thinking as our heart is thinking, instead of from any imagination of sin or mistake. Isaiah, the great prophet of the Old Testament, pictured a world in which the wolf and the lamb, the lion and the calf, shall lie down together, and the child shall play with the serpent, once more. This is the harmony of Truth.

There is nothing more miserable than to feel that by some mistake in life you have not amounted to what you might have, and that your misfortunes all hinge on that mistake. Some people who have made what they believe to have been mistakes don't affect their finances or environments through the consequences of their actions, but only their bodies or relationships. Some people's apparent mistakes touch their environment, while leaving their bodies hale and hearty.

But though a mistake may seem to be much, in Truth it is nothing. *God never made any mistakes in Spirit, so none of us can ever make mistakes in Spirit.* And as Spirit is all that is real of any of us, we must face any apparent troubles in our life with words that bring mistakes into nothing, troubles into nothing. This will not make them easier to bear; in fact, they will be gone.

Remember, Jesus taught that even our most vigorous belief in evil need not come forth in expression, for it is not real. So, if you have expressed some strong negative emotion, or some violent words fear not: they are not truth, and so have no power. As Jesus blasted the fig tree with no negative results, so you can never experience any fruits to bring hurt or misfortune from such momentary slips.

Learn that there is a divine harmony between the Mind out of which the true world is springing and your own mind — such harmony that you, yourself are that mighty and good Mind — and all the sting of all that seems to be hurtful shall be removed.

Once we feel, in our blood and bones, the Truth that we can never make a mistake, our fear will be gone. Inward buoyancy, kindled into speech dissolves the possibility of danger, animosity, and failure. Magnetic gladness of heart attracts gladness of heart. Therefore, "the joy of the Lord is your strength."

THE JOY-FILLED LIFE

The law of listening is the law of joy. Words caught from above always have healing and uplifting power

"Thy word was unto me the joy and rejoicing of my heart." Our joy is quickened from hearing the energizing Truth. The joy that comes from being in direct communication with the I AM increases us. The Old Testament teaches that Gideon and Abraham grew from non-entities to major figures in the history of Judaism as they learned to connect with the great I AM.

If we contemplate God within us, we shall find the God voice speaking within us, and it will be as audible as if it were outside us. For some, this voice may seem to come from outside, as it did to the Old Testament prophets. If we feel that God is around us, we may hear a voice from a bush, as Moses did, or from the air, as Samuel did. Or, we may hear a voice from the clouds as was heard at Jesus' baptism. If we are determined that God is ALL, we shall not be limited to the voice within or without, but everything will bear witness that we are in God. Then there is no seeking, no instruction to be firm: we are firm in our eternal Godhead and power.

But too many teachers and pastors have listened only to each other — how can pastors feed their followers with the joy of Goodness if they have not themselves been fed? How can their words be transforming if they hear only each others' thoughts?

The transforming words come from our looking and listening frequently toward the Heights of being. And their use increases our joy, for it is truly a joy to tell the words that transform the appearance of pain into peace and seeming disease into health.

Describing the strong and beautiful Self brings that power to here and now which is called healing. The Hindus call it animating the particular from the universal, the "particular" being the person or object on which we're focused. The right thought and word together activate the un-killable root of strength and vitality in all beings and things—giving life energy to whatever we speak to.

As our joy builds, it makes the hands magnetic to the angel of each person we encounter, pulling it forward as we extend our hand and say, "Come forth! It's God's will, it is your will, it is my will that you be well and strong and glad. Come forth!"

When we speak thus to the Soul, the Christ of a person, we are communicating with the Supernal, and at every turn we behold Divinity manifesting as beauty, health, joy, wisdom, and all the outward signs of the Universal Highest.

RECOGNITION & ACKNOWLEDGMENT

The great mystics have prophesied that the Messiah appears as the old "I" giving way to the new "I." They tell of the old "I" describing itself according to appearances and the new "I" telling the truth according to the kingdom of Heaven till it flashes its dominion over all that is.

As we acknowledge the Highest, the Great Countenance of the Absolute, the "I" Seed awakens in its location at the back of the breast, where it still lives in every breast upon earth. It sees. It feels. It knows. And It must cause us to show forth, brightening our paths with unprecedented, unforeseen, and unexpected Good. Heretofore hidden Truth comes boldly into view.

Recognition and acknowledgment are the "two-law" from which something must come forth. The old "I" gives way as we recognize the new, and "I decree" becomes our new song. Jesus touches the leper and says, "I will. Be thou clean." He threw away the old, appearance-bound "I" when he "called the woman to him and said unto her, 'Woman, thou art loosed from thine infirmity.'"

The ministry of recognition and acknowledgment to which we are called is wide and far reaching — though we may speak only to those at hand — for the "I' is universal, and at the same time, "very nigh unto thee." Francis Schlatter healed thousands of people by sensing that his God was near at hand, close by and encompassing, and that it was His will to heal through the willing Francis.

This metaphysical science of the recognition of the Presence of the divine in all is the oldest science of the human race — and the most effective. From Abram to Dante, the recognition of the divine precedes all else. A man known as "Old born drunk," who'd never had any will of his own, laid his hands on his breast, where the Celestial Spark glows in all of us, and said, "I am determined to find God." And all the criminals and debauched of his part of London went to their knees because the will-less sot did so! The young Joan of Arc, recognizing the divine Splendor, exclaimed, "I cannot retract — I am That!" And a nation still adores her.

EFFORTLESSNESS

As the lily is no less fragrant for all that a thousand people have smelled its scent, so the God Spark in each of us is never lessened. The "I am That" of myself and the "Thou art That" which I ardently proclaim to my neighbor, "scatters and yet increases." There is no limit to the joy of communing with the "I" that is stronger than Nature's forces and wiser than humanity's mind. Nor is there any delay; no time for dealing with possible blocks or delays. It stirs the victorious "I decree!" which came with us into this bodily form and nothing has greater power.

And as we focus on this, our Highest Self, our joy must come to pass, sooner or later.

If it is hard for you to accomplish an intention, or heal a case, you have been distracted by believing in hardship—for yourself or someone else. However, if you watch very carefully, you will see that there is no part of your life in which you are not guided by the Spirit into ways of pleasantness and peace. Any other perception is one you have chosen to experience, out of your mistaken understanding of others, yourself, or God. And a mistaken idea about God or about your own nature will most likely break out somewhere as distress in your experience.

This is why even students of Truth, claiming no belief in sin, sickness, or death, often do not immediately show peaceful, satisfied conditions. Just as the window pane that has been beaten with rain and dust for years is not clean just because the rain and dust have stopped, the mind is not immediately cleared of old habits of imagination. But practical daily washings of the dust of years are needed so that the old imaginings will seem less real.

Some, though, fret because it seems to take so long, and others seem to make life in the Spirit a burden. Too often, religious people make their lives harder for themselves and others. They rise early and stay up late, saying that as Spirit needs no rest and is strong enough to do all things, they are as able as Spirit to do that which is most harrowing—and expect as much of their whole family, without murmuring. You may be tempted to do the same.

But this is forgetting the way of Jesus, who slept, ate, drank, and clothed himself exactly like those around him—only doing differently when it pleased him. The yoke of the Christ Spirit is easy upon us. God is rest. The violets don't strain and struggle to be in harmony with their life. The mountains don't groan and labor to be great. The hurricanes and monsoons do their mighty tasks easily. Nor do we, because we are Spirit, need to think of life as hard. *Because we are Spirit, we do that which our own Wisdom prompts us to do*, laying no burdens on others out of our ideas.

GUIDELINES FOR TREATMENT

One treatment effectively manages our environment: "I do not accuse the world or myself of sin; all is well." God, as Truth, takes away any apparent distress and sickness and comforts all. God is merciful, so be merciful with yourself and those around you. The Good acts only through mercy.

You will be sure to have a patient or situation come around a third time if you have harbored feelings about how wrongly people have acted. Accusing others of selfishness or envy or jealousy or greed can be counted upon to do so.

By what right do we make such accusations? If Spirit is not any of these, then who are we talking about? Of nobody, most certainly, for Spirit is all! We are the Holy Spirit. If we call anybody malicious, sinful, revengeful, or cruel, we have spoken of Life, of

Mind, of Spirit—and that ties our own thoughts in chains so that we do not heal well, manage environments well, or do any of the things our thoughts must manage for us.

Within each of us is the joyful Song of the Spirit. As we think out the Song in our minds it breaks forth over all our affairs. Some Truth students sing their treatments, to express this inner Song more fully. You can sing mentally until a joy of the heart takes possession of your mind, and you will soon see this joy come to pass in happy surroundings.

Let us imagine nothing, therefore, but speak only Truth. Still, if we must imagine, then let us choose to imagine life, holy and omnipresent, conceiving only Omnipotent Good rather than any possibility of evil — in ourselves or others.

- Ω -

THE PRACTICE

On Wednesday afternoons, clear your own thoughts, saying the following until it feels real to you:

> I as Spirit do not accuse the world or myself of lust, greed, or attachment to material objects; all that I see and experience, everywhere I look, is good.

With a Returning Case:

Speak the case returning a third time by name. Stretch forth your invisible hands and urge the angel-self of this apparently sick person to make itself manifest, saying

> Come forth! It's God's will, and your will, and my will, that you be well and strong and glad! Come forth!

Speak forth your most joyous song; speak your most joyous text. Repeat it over and over until you feel completion.

Daily:

If you are fretting because it seems to take so long for your thoughts of good to come forth in your environment, repeat the following until it is a part of you:

> I give thanks and glad praise that the Creator has given the Spirit all the joy and song of the universe, and so Spirit, which I am, need never pray for joy, nor beg for it, nor work for it, nor struggle for it. The Spirit that I AM is joyous and sings because Spirit is joy. I am glad that the Holy Spirit of me is joy and harmony—here, now, always, and everywhere.

[These words are suggestions, only; feel free to use whatever similar words are inspired within you.]

THE METAPHORS

The Number: NINE

Nine was, to the ancient Greeks, the number of enchantment, not to be spoken aloud. It was too likely to hit the Super "I" at the back of the chest, behind the solar plexus, and to speak forth from that "I" would be to wish those words on someone or something. The number nine, to the Romans, was the tangibility of angels.

Nine is our joy in our own responsive God center. Nine is the Assumption, the Joyful Magnificat of Mary, the taking for granted, or supposing something without visible proof. Nine stands for the closing of an old cycle and the opening of a new one; the old touching the new and the new touching the old like beads on a rosary. The Bible states that, at the crucifixion, the sun was darkened from the sixth to the ninth hour, and at the ninth hour Jesus gave up the ghost. Hebrew law said that a farmer should eat the old harvest until the ninth month, and some prophecies said that the Messiah would come in the ninth cycle.

The Stone: Topaz

The true topaz is extremely valuable. It signifies that the triumph of steadfast vision has come in the form of words that set nobility where wickedness was seen before—as Joseph's steadfast long vision and speech transformed his murderous brothers into lovers in Egypt. The ninth stone in the breastplate of the Hebrew high priest symbolizes the tribe of Dan, or harmony between thoughts and externals—the peace and delight with the way we are walking that comes with acceptance.

The Apostle: Andrew, Strength.

The English form of the Greek name, *Andreas*, Andrew means "strong, manly," from the Greek root, *andros*, meaning "man." It's probable that the Hebrew name of this disciple was *Enash* or *Enowsh*, from the Chaldean root *Enos*, meaning "man," "a son of Adam," or possibly *Anath*, meaning, "answering, shouting, announcing, bearing witness," Andrew's words being the Spirit's response to the cry of the soul for deliverance. Andrew is the one who proclaimed "We have found the Messiah!"

Andrew symbolizes strength, while his brother, Simon Peter, symbolizes faith. When strength finds faith, a bond of unity is established that carries one along regardless of apparent circumstances. The day when you, by the sight of God at your center, recognize that all you experience is the spreading forth of your own divine essence, you are opened on the Andrew side and can never feel pain any more.

Lesson Ten: Effectiveness—Freedom from Fear

The tenth lesson of metaphysical Science applies the principle of the fourth lesson: "mind will demonstrate as much Truth as it has courage to stand by its affirmations" — to our environment. This lesson gives us the gift of skill in handling things with our thoughts so they record our thoughts perfectly. Its axiom is similar: the world will persist in exhibiting before you what you persist in affirming that the world is. It teaches us to make our work effective, making it as definitely good, and as alive in its good, as in our own soul.

A musical instrument records perfectly the joy of the master musician by vibrating at the touch of the masterly fingers, and that musician's skill can be recorded. Paganini could make the violin send forth tones and semi-tones of harmonies hitherto unheard of by humankind, yet there is no record of his harmonies: he had no skill in instructing others in his science.

Your practice, though, must tell the world what your inner Genius can do. Everything you do must, by its very nature, have its clear process that shows others how to do likewise. It's not to your credit to heal blindness or whatever suddenly and, so to speak, "accidentally." You must know how to heal when you heal, be able to teach others how to heal, and keep your cases well after they are healed. You must know how to make a permanent work.

The number ten is a beginning in fullness, so this tenth lesson teaches us to start over again at our hidden *memra,* our Secret Self, and sound our song out loud until the earth shall hear and repeat the anthem, singing with the choirs of Revelation, "We give thee thanks because thou hast taken to thyself thy great power and hast reigned."

If we have discovered how to be joyous and grateful here on earth, which sometimes seems so dark and unreliable; if we have learned to smile and praise when there was nothing, seemingly, to smile or be grateful about, there will come a moment when everything we are able to do we can teach others to do.

The risen Jesus said that the Holy Ghost would teach us all things. Men have studied books and languages, machines and all creation, but they have not practiced learning from the Holy Spirit. That Spirit is in yourself, residing at your core; let it always think and speak through you. Remember what Moses heard, when he was sent to free the Israelites from Egypt: "Now therefore go, and I will be with thy mouth and teach thee what thou shalt say." The silent language of wordless knowing deep within us comes to our speech as we recognize that hidden center where the Inmost Lord and the Highest Lord is one Lord.

SHAPING THE WORLD

Things and objects and people around us are the records now of ways we have thought and spoken in the past and how we are thinking and speaking now. Everything and everyone is as good to us as we have been to it or them. They record our skill. They tell of our ability to put our Soul's Life into words. They tell of our ability to discard appearance and recognize reality, while we are thinking, speaking, and writing.

Moses said, "Let the earth bring forth cattle and creeping things." Earth, here, means mind in its persistent thought. "Cattle" is a symbol for social systems, such as governments, schools, or families. "Creeping things" refers to the daily tasks of eating, sleeping, drinking, etc.. These things come forth in a new beauty with the persistent thinking of new truths, which are like cheerful breaths of the Spirit.

All the world, including our close family relations, are Good beyond good. If we use the Good Mind in us, how can we help seeing the Truth of the world? Let the mind see the good, step by step. From mountain peak to mountain peak, let these lofty ideas spring, till the twelve gates of Truth are opened and our conscious, wide-awake thoughts, never off guard, smile and rejoice that our obedient world may be at last compelled to return our smile.

Gentleness, love, cheerfulness — these may seem slow to conquer the world, but they have Deity, in all its force, behind them. Any one idea of Good, held in mind, is a deathless seed. If it is in mind, it is in your body and affairs, also, for what you are thinking about is surely in your surroundings. So today, Moses would say, "Stand here and see your mighty Principle carried out in your governments, churches, schools, homes, friends, family life, and into your daily tasks, eating, drinking, and sleeping. Let everything that has breath or moves sing praise to the Lord within us all."

When we think new and joyous thoughts of people, of things, of life, they begin to respond to our thoughts. The joyousness you've persisted in has recorded itself in them, and answers back to you, as in a mirror. When they do so, it's a credit to your skill —

quite different from having things seem mysteriously good, or unexpectedly kind.

When anyone imagines that there is a mixture of good and evil in the universe, they're sure to see a great deal of both good and evil. If they let their mind balance on the gloomy side, more than on the joyous side, they will see more evil conditions than good in the world. They're not touching the tenth lesson—they'll not see the world record joyousness—if they don't put joyousness forth from their mind as a steady stream into the world.

If Spirit is the only substance, then matter is no substance; if Holiness is the only presence, sin cannot be present; if omniscience is omnipresent, there can be no ignorance. We must truly not see any faults in our neighbors, nor ignorance nor foolishness hiding their innate wisdom. There is one Good Mind, and when accusation is laid aside, all who are wise render the same verdict as to what is true.

Permanent Healing

If we talk of healing the sick, we don't mean that there are sick people, but that we see people more and more nearly as they truly are. If we speak of casting out tempers or passions (or "demons," as they are referred to in the Bible), we don't mean that there truly are demons or tempers or overwhelming passions, but that we see the Holy Spirit in each person, instead of such things. There is no death; we see life where others believe in death.

When you cure your case by this Wisdom, it is cured for all eternity. He or she cannot have that malady again.

To heal someone of their mental formulations, called disease, you simply disintegrate their accumulated ideas by True thoughts. You reason those ideas right out of their mind. It's very much like ungluing them: the old ideas fall all to pieces and there's nothing left of them.

In the process, there's always a little moment when it almost seems as if someone would not let the old ideas go. If, at that moment, you are true to Principle, stronger than ever, and ignore any conditions with more skill than ever, you will see the false position yielded without another struggle.

A very lame man was at a meeting when slavery was called a "divine institution." This so upset him and stirred his mind that it held his body free from lameness and he jumped to his feet. But when the people laughed to see him forget his lameness, he remembered it again and sat down, as lame as ever. By contrast, when a woman who was being healed kept shouting how much worse she was, the healer took even less notice of her than before, praising God in her secret mind with more intense praises than ever, till the patient ceased screaming and, after a few moments cried, "I am entirely healed!"

The prophet Joab once told the Israelite people that they shouldn't count their soldiers, because it would have discouraged them to know what a small army they had. So sometimes it's best not to think how your patient is, not to ask him a single question, not to talk to her at all, not even to answer any questions. Keep your mind only on one side of the argument: keep it on the side of your faith and ignore the rest. "I don't believe a word of it—not a word," you say while he mourns or she cries or complains or describes her ailments.

If business troubles face you after you have treated faithfully three treatments, you certainly have been doubtful whether you could settle them by mental processes or not. Doubt is sure to haul a once-lame business back into lameness again. You need to refuse the lameness. Don't touch it. "Touch not the earth," means to keep your eye on the highest Truth.

Say to your affairs, if they keep facing you with what looks like disaster, "I don't believe it! I don't believe that side of the question. I believe in success and prosperity—for myself and everyone else!" You say it to all that troubles you. You say it to anything that comes for a fourth time, and every Thursday afternoon.

The old conditions must unglue; they must go. Good reigns. Believe it.

OUR PERFECT GIFT

You know there's a natural strength within your mind to be your best and do your most creditable thing. You choose to do and be success. Some have chosen to be known as very rich; they would have that as their high ambition. Some have chosen to lead society life in New York City, London, or Paris. Mendelssohn chose to be known by his "Elijah" in music. The Renaissance painter Raphael will always be known as "Divine" because of "The Transfiguration." Each of us has a particular achievement to accomplish.

Paul said, "Every man has his proper gift of God," and told his helper, Timothy, to churn up the gift that was in him. In the same way, the thoughts brought forth by repeating the lessons of this Science will stir up your own gift. They'll open a way for you to exercise that gift, and everything will yield to that gift stirred up in you.

We learned in an earlier lesson that the waters form the land. The land, once formed, must take great and unusual force by the waters to change its shape and appearance. This metaphysical Science teaches that the land of your being is your present conditions, your circumstances—may even be called your fate. So the waters of your mind must form your natural world. Whatever you've thought consciously, the conditions of your life must unresistingly record.

At the height of your unique genius rests some masterpiece of splendor, laid out for you to do from the beginning, before ever the world was formed. It is the making of your soul, your own Christ character whose glory rests ever in the center of your own being, manifesting in your own world. And through this Science your mind is a greater work than Mendelssohn's, for there is music far beyond his masterpiece, but there can be no music beyond that which you bring forth from the earth when you have proved that, to you, there is only the Truth of Good. Things are a changeable substance that your skillful thoughts mold, as Michelangelo molded plaster, bronze, and marble. The world is as receptive to your touches as the canvas was to Leonardo DaVinci.

CHOOSING FAITH OVER DOUBT OR FEAR

If you have thought seriously about some great point in this Science for a long time, you will experience its mighty effects. The "land" that is your circumstances is undermined, disintegrated, dissolved, by your new, true way of thinking. All the opposition of your human nature and experience, your habits of thought and disposition, will meet your statement, somewhere, and a new form must take shape.

Though true thought may seem, sometimes, to be long in accomplishing its mission, still our conscious thoughts get greater and greater power as we think them, till our whole earth falls apart. We don't believe in the old material ways of thinking anymore, so old conditions, manufactured by our old material thoughts have unglued, as they must in order that our new conditions, formulated by our new way of thinking may come forth. At this point, friends change amazingly; our home is transformed; our business falters—perhaps even appearing to fail.

But we need not fear: at this point we are at the cave, the sepulcher in the beautiful garden of resurrection. We need not say, "They have taken away my Lord!" simply because things look as if they were failing us. Instead, we must look up, up—and touch not the earth, touch God! In our interior God-point, we see as God sees and know as God knows, and in Reality, all is Paradise.

This is the point of choice where our old beliefs about God come forth. It may seem as if our world all turns against us. But we have no right to agree with what appears around us. The Christ Spirit within us is shedding its radiance around us, and there's no combination of circumstances so hard, so black, so complicated, that God's Spirit cannot work a miracle in them. No matter what part of our circumstances seems to be falling apart, there is a spiritual place—eternal, not materially thought, not materially born, but spiritually brought forth — now showing its seed, its face, through the ungluing particles of the old conditions.

Whenever any disturbed condition arises, do not believe in it enough to notice it. Behind you, over you, near you, within you, is a voice saying, "Touch not the earth, touch Me." So you look away from your situation, and with the simple assertion, "I do not believe in evil or distress; I believe only in Good!" put your mind entirely on the Spirit that is all-that-is. All acute cases, of sickness or any distress, are simply signals for you to declare firmly what you do believe and what you do not.

Sometimes, when "the earth comes unglued" after you've decided to put forth cheerfulness, the unbalanced and distracted state of your affairs may seem to make it impossible for you to hold your own in the midst of your seemingly disordered world. When the storms seem to come thickest, the peace of your soul is nearest. We have only to look away from the turmoil. If we are steadfast in standing by the central spark, the I AM that never dies within us, fear will take flight. "Thou shalt not fear," is prophecy, not command.

"Be steadfast," said Paul. "Praise without ceasing," was his recommendation. All metaphysicians have agreed that the sanctuary at our core is indestructible, "the rock of mine heart," for all mankind. Nothing resists the firm inward maintenance of the rock-centered Truth. Choose faith.

All metaphysicians who've been strong and steadfast have seen everything change around them, simply because they have so entirely changed their thoughts. Holding steadfast to one Principle, they have passed through seeming trials with ease, to victory. Once a woman had so much trouble that she felt she was losing her mind. She said, "I do not believe it is Thy will that I should be in trouble." Over and over, she repeated Isaiah's promise: "Thou wilt keep him in perfect peace whose mind is stayed on Thee," till help came to her. She was saved, not only mentally, but her conditions righted themselves as well.[64]

You can't help but notice how chilling and depressing doubt can be. It may come up and shake you. Many call their doubt of the Good now working itself out in their lives, fear. Some call it "the blues." By whatever name, it's simply the shadow cast by the figure of Faith, which stands so near you. She can do anything: raise your hopes to highest heaven, fulfill your dearest wish. She is warming and strengthening—comforting. You can choose her at any time, or you can choose doubt; one is the reality, the other imagination; and one or the other is chosen by what you say most vehemently in your heart.

I have heard of people giving in so fully to their doubts and fears that they could only struggle feebly to lay hold of Faith. The fact is you have to choose Faith the first thing: your future is determined by your initial, heart-felt response.

But choosing Faith is not pretending that what distresses you must somehow be Good. That's a mistake too many students of metaphysics make. This Science does not say that death is good; it says there is no death. This Science does not say that poverty is good;

---

[64] Probably another autobiographical incident—possibly referring to the "falling apart" when Emma was dismissed from her position with Mrs. Eddy's school and church.

it says there is no poverty. This Science does not say that changing ugly conditions is good; it says only good conditions are Real. Such attempts to make misery and death and poverty good turn the principle upside down. They do not exist; they're not real; so how can they be Good?

That which is present, is, by definition, Good. So, if any situation seems to distress, there's no point in trying to "find the Good in it." Say, rather, that it never transpired. Do not speak to any person about it, speak to God. See God's Good presence only. "Only one is Good," said Jesus, "and that is God."

If you tell me that your husband was such-and-such, your money was such-and-such, or your children were so-and so, and you cannot say they are good conditions, then you have arrived at this important lesson on your journey in the metaphysical Science. You must not think of a single one of these appearances. They are not there at all. Where you thought they were, God is there: the only reality. Touch not the earth with your mind, touch only the infinite I AM.

If, as your "earth comes unglued," you see only disheartening circumstances, you will find it most comforting to say, "I do not believe in the power of even a whole army of evil conditions; I believe God, all-powerful, is bringing all through safely." If you feel the shakiness of fear, you can say, "There is nothing to fear; I am embraced by the loving God." You can say, "I believe in the loving God here present; I will not doubt the Good."

Why should you write to your mother, or uncle, or brother, begging for help out of your apparent misery, when the whole universe is waiting for you to touch, not the earth, but God? This is called "the valley of decision," and people are so inclined to speak of hardships that the prophet Joel spoke of the "multitudes, multitudes, in the valley of decision." This is the lonely valley of despair—if you choose to see it so. But you, as a student of this metaphysical Science, see beyond appearances and choose Faith. You "touch not the earth; touch Me."

TIME

Chances are that any doubt and fear you feel is not so much a doubt of the Good, as a fear that the Good won't work NOW. Our culture teaches that the Good lets evil run on so long, and that multitudes of good people pass away before their good deeds are respected, and ages go on before their character is believed in. Many of us have the sneaking feeling, what good will it do us if our wrongs are not set right at this very moment?

Come, face up to this adversary. Its name is a belief in time: that it takes time for the Good to work, that God takes a long time to work out our cause for us. What can I expect but the passage of time, if I believe in it? What can I expect but fear if I believe in fear? All these things are my own imaginations worked out in my experience. In Truth, all is Good, NOW.

Did you ever see people who, when they were in what appeared to be great trouble, never touched it with their thoughts, but touched only the Good? Anybody who faces up to that little sneaking fear that it would take a long time to set their affairs straight by saying, "I am not going to believe that the Almighty needs an instant of time to bring forth right conditions here and now!" must have their needs met.

EXPERIENCING JOY AND PEACE

All the lessons of metaphysical Science turn us toward joy and peace. Jesus, the master metaphysician, was so cheerful and joyous that he was called a glutton and wine-bibber by those who taught the "straight and narrow" path, and his joyful disciples were accused of being drunk. He was so full of confidence in the good of all people that the pious ones were distressed at his association with people of bad reputation. He was so firm on the side of Good in all that, even as he lived in apparent poverty and lack, He owned the universe and proclaimed the immanence of Heaven.

Whoever follows this Science soon discovers that something about himself is healed, even as he or she works to heal others. You'll find that, even now, you can point to ways that you are better for having studied this Science. You may choose more such healing, and treat for yourself as you do for others. Deny that any cause, or result of any kind, leading to folly, sickness, or trouble, has ever existed in your life. Claim your life in Spirit and the Comforter will teach you all things needful.

So the tenth lesson, with its metaphors, is for you to know that you are a transcendent being with transcendent powers. You were born of God. You go toward God, you know God; you have the power of God. It's the same with any case that comes to you: each one is a transcendent being coming into your sight. It's the same with your circumstances: they are Paradise coming into view.

Apparent evil is always just a signal to welcome the Spirit, to see as God sees, and to step into a higher Truth. Sometimes a physical or mental disturbance arises when Truth is spoken, as the effect of an old opposition to the Truth. It may look like all sorts of physical or mental disease. This is called "chemicalization." It, too, is a sign — that Truth is working fast and that we are to welcome the Spirit's action in our lives. If, for example, our friend seems to take a fever, or fall down in a faint, we speak rapidly and with feeling: "I do not believe in sickness, fainting or failure; I believe in life and activity!" We stand with confidence, assurance, and certainty, reaching for that everlasting health that shines back of any apparent distress and can brush aside any symptoms, as the sun sweeps away the clouds.

Whenever such seemingly evil conditions appear, we don't have to do anything about them — only to feel the presence of Good above them. A case of a child's diphtheria, for example, is not diphtheria at all, but a signal to you that, by the right words now spoken you can bring forth a perfect character renewed intelligence, and beautiful health into your world. So you say, promptly, from the heart, "I do not believe in any illness! I believe in the Holy Spirit working. I believe in peaceful health manifest in everyone present, here and now!"

There may be times when circumstances will not yield till after we've been so powerfully absorbed in our Principle that we forget all about everything else, as with the mother who went down on her knees for money to send her boy to school. She arose on the third day, her face radiant with the mental assurance of an answer, and that very day the money came. Jesus told his disciples that they could not cure a case of epilepsy except by praying so earnestly that they forgot to eat — because that's what it would take to overcome their belief in the power of demons.

The Truth is that all creatures of the earth are obedient records of your conscious calling of their true names, and as you master this artful Science, you'll find the secret Selves of every creature and make them speak. The Self of the stone is its God life. When that's plainly visible to your awareness, it is visible forever.

This is why Jesus taught that we can quell the roughness of a stormy ocean or mighty winds by sending our steady words of peace over the waters. They will respond. Even the disturbed waters of many minds respond to our thoughts of peace: a public brawl was quelled by the silent thoughts of a metaphysical Scientist who sat peacefully on the edges, never looking up, but saying "It's nothing at all, peace is here. I do not believe in disturbance; I believe in harmony."

The more often we bring order out of such chaos, ignoring such apparently mixed-up states of affairs, the more we build our effectiveness in this Science. To stand still and hold on to a Principle when another statement seems to control the situation is to become a skillful artist, approved by heaven. The woman who is on the point of bankruptcy and saves herself by this Science touches this lesson, and proves her effectiveness with this Science. The person whose eyesight seems to fail and, though all treatments seem only to put them into deeper darkness, holds on to one principle until it pulls them into light, must see that everything will yield to ongoing treatment; difficulties never daunt such a person.

The world is obedient to your confidence, your faith, and your steadfast ignoring of any doubts or fears or appearances. So, when Truth goes singing over your thoughts, there is nothing to fear, no pain, and no sorrow, for Truth does not concern itself with any such illusory circumstances.

GUIDELINES FOR TREATMENT

Nothing can push your patient's cure out of your sight but your own doubts and fears. If you're remembering how sick your patient looks, you must turn that memory right around by looking at a picture of some lofty being, or speaking lofty principles over and over, for your memory of how your patient seemed while sick will bring out that sickness plainly into your experience.

This is where you must state that you believe your Principle is working itself in its own way, and that there can be nothing working against Principle. Again, choose Faith, declaring with intensity what you believe and what you do not.

Cases returning are simply the exposure of some doubts you yourself have been having, which you could have canceled immediately with, "I BELIEVE ONLY IN THE GOOD."

Your fear need not be of your patient's sickness, nor even that you will fail; you could be afraid that your family's affairs won't come out right, and it will be enough to bring a condition back for the fourth time.

If a patient, or an issue, comes before you a fourth time for healing, it shows that you had been disturbed about whether good or evil is more powerful in the world before they called. Maybe you'd been wondering if, after all, maybe there was a Satan, or "an axis of evil." Maybe you had thought it might be so, in the long run, that good and right and justice would prevail, but at present things were pretty dark. Things must have seemed very much mixed up to you, for such conflict to be going on within your patient's mind and body or affairs.

Well, the first thing to do is to bow the head and let the Sprit speak of confidence, faith, and steadfastness. You've come to Paul's "middle wall of partition," where you must let the Spirit speak through you, reminding you the Truth of your Principle: "I do not believe in mixtures of good and evil. I do not believe in failure; I believe only in success."

- Ω -

THE PRACTICE

Thursday Afternoons:

We will take Thursday to regard our neighbor "at the temple" within our hearts, our hidden meeting place with God, agreeing with the angel standing there, and seeing the health and well-being that is that person's Truth. We will also take the ones we love best into that place.

If you will take Thursday afternoons and say all that the Spirit does not believe and all that the Spirit does believe, you will not have a long treatment with a case that appears the fourth time. Try saying:

I have not believed in a mixture of good and evil. I do not believe in evil of any kind; I believe that all is Good.

There is no reality in trouble; all is peace.

There is no reality in sickness; all is perfect health.

I do not believe in anything wrong; I believe all is well.

With a Returning Client

Call the name of the situation or person who has come a fourth time, and let the Spirit in you speak the ideas below:

There is no mixture of good and evil in you; all is Good.

I don't believe in inheritance of any kind of sickness, disease, or pain. I believe in the inheritance of God's Good only.

I don't believe in a humanity that is partly good and partly evil; I believe in the universality of Good.

I don't believe in contagion by the mixed thoughts of people around us; I believe in their Good Mind only.

I don't believe in any evil thoughts in your mind; your mind is Good.

I don't believe in any errors in you or me; such do not exist; all is Good.

You are every whit whole and experience only well-being.

Your life is God; it can't be threatened with disease, nor fear disease, nor yield to disease in any part of your being.

Your strength is God; it can't be threatened with weakness, nor fear weakness, nor yield to weakness in any part of your being.

You are demonstrating to the people around you that you are healed. You acknowledge to yourself that you are healed. You acknowledge to me that you are healed.

In the name of the Father/Mother Almighty, the Miracle-working Heir, and the Mystical Holy Breath of Spirit Present I now pronounce you healed, forever and ever, for it is so.

[These words are suggestions, only; feel free to use whatever similar words are inspired within you.]

You will see good health stand out very plainly, right then and there. And if you repeat it over and over, you will be so confident of the Good and right coming forth, that nothing can distract your attention at all. By such treatments as this you will see the whole world healed of grief, sickness and pain, of poverty and error.

THE METAPHORS

The Number: TEN

Ten is the number of the Light, giving birth to everything. Ten is the number of the *memra* of the mystics, the secret word of the Mystic Self. Ten is the I AM. Aristotle, in 384 B.C.E., found that there are but ten ideas in the world, as there are but ten numbers. All the religions and philosophies of the world are but variations of these ten ideas, as all of mathematics are variations on the ten numbers.

"With ten words was the world built," reads the ancient Zoroastrian text, the Zend Avesta. The ancient Hebrews declared that the tenth letter of the alphabet, Yod, is key to the divine language that must sometime come forth from the hidden "I" of the heart — with all the angels, authorities, and powers subject to that divine language.

Ten is the fulfillment, the completion. Ten is the Rose of the World, the Sephiroth, come into bloom. It is the number of empowerment, the Great Resurrection, calling our attention to our native majesty. By the law of Ten we take back the lordship that we had given to defeat, deafness, death; we take back the power that we gave others to hurt our feelings; we take back the authority we'd given to poverty, inconsequence, and ignorance. Ten is the jubilee day, "and the people came up out of the Jordan on the tenth day, ...cause the trumpet of the jubilee to sound on the tenth day..."

The Stone: Chrysoprasus,

A variety of chalcedony, chrysoprasus is apple green in color. It is the color that stands for the true earth, the Heavenly City called the New Jerusalem that descends, the Holy bride who will be the wife of the Lamb—the green fields and gleaming mountains of paradise. The chrysoprasus stands for dauntlessness: understanding how to handle things without effort. It is the stone of companionship, of dwelling among equals, of seeing the Good where others see evil, of speaking of God's blessed kindness in the face of apparent bitterness. In the priest's breastplate, it is turquoise, standing for the tribe of Naphtali, meaning "overcoming the dark."

The Apostle: John, God's Grace.

John is the English translation of the Greek *Ioannes* (I is used instead of J in Greek and Latin), which is translated from *Jachanan* in Hebrew, meaning "favored by Jehovah" or "revived by Jehovah." John is the assumed author of the Gospel of John, which is the most mystical account of the life and teachings of Jesus the Nazarene, which opens with, "In the beginning was the Word and the Word was with God and the Word was God." Tradition says that he is also the author of the Book of Revelation, the final vision of the Bible, written on the island of Patmos about 90 C.E., but most scholars agree that the language and style are of a different writer. Traditions around the Mediterranean suggest that John the Disciple never died, but was translated into his light body and comes into human form in various places on certain dates.

John is associated with the base chakra, above the navel, which in Asia is the chi point, where universal energy enters the body.

The Beatitude for John is, "Rejoice and be exceeding glad, for great is your reward in heaven…"

Lesson Eleven: The Way of Wisdom

In the last lesson, we were shown the importance of holding our highest thoughts, even while the client's condition gives the appearance of holding onto evil. The eleventh lesson addresses the situation where it seems as if your premise or Principle, which has pleased you so much, is, after all, much feebler than the premise of the patient who claims to be sick.

Sometimes, after taking a premise, there comes a time when it seems as if it could never work. If you've become shaken up, and fallen back to your old thoughts, you must quickly declare new affirmations, from a warm sense of understanding, or the world will set itself to the old tune again. Paul said, "Stand, and having done all, stand." He also said that God can help us stand firm to our premise, once we've taken it, because those who've recognized that within them is God, must live the life that knowledge opens for them—we can never go back to affirming evil once we have seen the Good in all.

The strongest position you can take is always on the side of happiness and peace, as they are the Reality of our lives. If someone tells you they are well, and you cheerfully and innocently believe them, even when medical tests have suggested otherwise, they will be recovered by your faith. This is because confidence, or Faith, is a life principle. As God cannot fail, these cannot fail.

If you grasped the tenth lesson, you know what to do in the face of apparent distress: you persist as hard as the circumstances do, only you persist in ignoring it and living on your side of the question, that of peace and happiness and well-being. Persistence is a wonderful manager.

If you find it difficult to imagine holding to your Principle, try imagining vast openings and channels of power. Try thinking that being true to your idea will be like getting so much wealth straight from the Spirit of God, that you can feed all the seemingly poor people of the world; so much health straight from the Spirit of God that you can heal all the apparent disease in the world; so much wisdom straight from the Spirit of God that you can guide all the seemingly dark minds of the world into the light.

Of course, you know this is only a mode of expressing the Truth: by your own Wisdom you will experience wisdom around you, by your own Health you will see only health in others, and by your own acknowledgment of Infinite Provision, you experience bounty everywhere.

WILL & MEEKNESS

This eleventh lesson has for its axiom: Judgment is as great and competent as will and meekness can agree. You have a strong will. Naturally, you feel like having everything go your own way, and this is good, as long as you are willing to yield your point the instant you see your way doesn't work. Wisdom is to be found in the combination of these two qualities: your mind will unconsciously protect your strong will, so it won't be yielding to another's quick judgment of a situation, while you will be consciously directing your will along the highest path, so far as you can see it.

We may count on it that we've used our will to carry out our own notions, right or wrong — or that we've yielded ourselves to doing something we lacked a will to do — if we come to a point of indecision. Whenever we come to a point where we don't quickly know what to do, we are in an unbalanced condition of mind, called foolishness or ignorance. These always come from carrying out our own will, regardless of everything, and ignoring our higher judgment, rather than meekly accepting it.

You can make the most divine decisions by compelling your meekness to unite with your will. If, for example, things were to look poorly for your business, do you will them to be bad? No! A thousand times no! Your will is for the Good, but your will cannot carry the day alone; it must be married to meekness. Meekness means yielding to the spiritual principle, even when appearances seem to argue louder than Reality.

The word, "meekness," has gotten a good many religious people into misery. It seemed to them to mean yielding to evil and difficulties of appearances. A young man found he'd been thinking he must yield to his poverty as sent by God. He quickly saw his mistake: God does not send poverty! Whoever has said that the bountiful Creator-Sustainer of the universe is a giver of poverty has lied. He had been badly tempted, and foolishly yielded to the temptation to judge against his will, falling on the side of appearances. Solomon said, "The foolishness of man perverts his way." Way is another word for will.

All weakness of the body comes from yielding to appearances instead of holding to metaphysical understandings. Therefore, when someone comes asking for help from weakness, you know that the key-stone to touch is foolishness and ignorance, which are nothing in the presence of omniscience. So you can easily say, "Your will never fell to temptation."

The doctrine of "the Fall of Humanity" came from believing in the reality of temptation, and of material appearances. But it is false. Our will never fell through temptation. Will is another name for God, the Good, and God cannot fall nor fail. Nor does God tempt us into evil — since evil cannot exist in omnipresent Good.

In ancient times a lamb, the symbol of trust and meekness, was sent into the wilderness with ribbons signifying all the sins of the village tied into its wool. "Behold the Lamb of God, which taketh away the sins of the world." The Lamb of God refers to the Christ — manifest in Jesus the Nazarene and present in all of us — who condemned none, forgave all, suspected no one, believed in no evil, feared nothing, and loved everything. Therefore, he healed instantly, and could say, "All power has been given unto Me in Heaven and in Earth."

The perfect in judgment are perfect in beauty. The beauty of Jesus is because his judgment was polished by meekness. Jesus is bound by no traditions: what others believed he must be in order to be beautiful, he need not believe. What own good judgment claims becomes charm.

So marry your will to the facts of the case. Rouse your judgment, the animus, or "man" in you. Moses said, "Let us make man... and let him have dominion." Jesus said, "The Father hath committed all judgment unto the Son," meaning the Divine Heir in each of us. Your own mind must be this inheritor having dominion. Your own judgment must reign supreme, as it has no evil before it.

If you see symbols, speak of their good for your surroundings; they all come for your benefit. No matter what others believe about the meaning of your dream of the night, you must judge that it means something good for your surroundings — whether others might call it evil or not. Your judgment yielding only to the good sees and says that some blessed good is coming to you.

And when you consistently lay your judgment to the plumb-line of the highest truths you've heard, then, says the prophet of Revelation, your old covenant with death will be annulled and your agreement with hell will not stand. You give up your old ideas in meekness, and you speak aloud your new ideas with conviction, having thought them and written them.

The more you speak according to this judgment, the more judgment your neighbors will have. They may not see at first that you are wise with the Divine Mind, from which you are drinking daily as you work through these twelve lessons, but after a time your ideas will be recognized and others will acknowledge the excellence of your judgment.

DEMONSTRATION & REDEMPTION

These ideas are the new growth in good soil, so let them sink into the deep soil of profound meditation. Their fruits are light, if lightly handled, but by the deep thought of the mind, the word of the lips is ripe and heavy with the perfect fruit of solid judgment.

Demonstration is the result of judgment. One often finds that demonstration waits for him to give up prejudices with respect to what is high or low. Lofty ambitions are evidence of a belief in high and low places. But all must be alike to the practitioner of this Science, for all are descriptions of Spirit and there is neither high nor low in Spirit. So they who believe in high or low will have to take some statement which to them seems low, in order to attain the perfect judgment that will accomplish their intention.

Practicing this Science will bring you to see that you are not unsuccessful, no matter how unsuccessful you may appear to your old way of thinking, because Spirit is never unsuccessful. The instant your judgment is accurate with respect to success and non-success, all things will work out to your pleasure, even in the old way of looking at them.

In the Gospel, or "good news" of this Science, there is no material remedy for disease. This is because, while in the law, disease seems very real and Truth is its remedy, in the Gospel there is no disease, so not even Truth heals. So when wise judgment is come forth, you find that you're not bound to methods of curing the sick, or even eating, drinking, sleeping, or dressing. Reality is simply exposed in your presence.

As judgment ripens with yielding the will to these lessons of this Science over and over again, you'll see great events and circumstances yielding to very simple actions on your part. Whoever thinks anything is terrible must certainly believe in it greatly. It must have great power in their eyes. They may have to take medication to see how unreal it is, how simply dealt with, how far from terrible. But in Truth nothing is terrible; nothing is to be hated.

Even stealing must not be hated. Why? Well, what is stealing? Isn't it a delusion of imagination? Isn't God the only being? Can God steal from God's own self? Thinking in this way awakens the mind to Truth and wise judgment will result in some potential thief finding another source of support.

PERFECT JUDGMENT

Effective judgment comes of compelling yourself to believe just as much as you hope for. One man felt suddenly, after long practice in this Science, that he could as easily make gold as cure bones, but a voice seemed to say to him, "You would act foolishly with gold if you had it." He yielded the point at once, thinking that it looked meek to yield to a warning voice. But no voice from the Spirit ever accuses a mind of foolishness or ignorance. Instead, here was one of his own self-accusations, blooming in order to be refused by his will, so that his greatest hopes might be fulfilled.

Once in a while you may find that nothing you do yourself causes your patient's cure: so far as you see, they get their cure by reason of somebody else's treatments, after you have treated them. Or, you may find that money is not given you to pay off some debt, yet, somehow, by some deal or other, no debt remains. This is the result of your will being married to a kind of weak yielding to the statements of this Science. You didn't make them your deep life, or your solid assistance.

Isaiah told the people of Israel (which means "children of God," and includes us all), when they'd gotten themselves into captivity through careless speaking of their Science, that they would wish for money to redeem themselves, but they would be redeemed, not with money — only by their fidelity to the truths of their spiritual teachings. Isaiah's words, "Ye have sold yourselves for a thing of naught, and ye shall be redeemed" are spoken to any half-hearted, insincere, timid, unprofound acceptance of this Science. Even writing these ideas glibly brings out the redemption, but without substantial, solid aid. Even thinking these words will do the same.

But living them comes from thinking this Science deeply, writing honestly, and speaking sacredly, and when the outward life is in accord with Principle, then judgment is risen in her beauty. Then healing is instantaneous. Then, when help is needed, it comes exactly as your perfect judgment would indicate.

Perfect judgment touches the life chords of each situation with the right word. The mind must agree with the Spirit; the law and the Gospel must be one; hope and faith must be wed. Then comes perfect judgment, and the keys of heaven and earth are given to perfect judgment.

The refusal to call any man, woman, or child foolish or ignorant will uncover the dormant chord of your will. The strings of your soul will then be exposed for the breath of God to blow upon and bring out the glorious tones, the radiant beauty, given unto your judgment from the foundations of the universe.

The point is to get your perfect judgment forward. It comes forward by handling this eleventh lesson. Its signal is the need for a fifth treatment. So, whenever the occasion arises, we say, "I never accuse the world or myself of foolishness or ignorance. I am the discerning judgment of God. I know all things and do all things well."

If you and I don't speak from our spiritual Self, it will not act through us or for us. The Buddha taught that the spiritual Self is Lord over the human self. The Old Testament teaches that it's good to tame the human mind, which is very flighty, rushing hither and thither, but once tamed brings great happiness.

INSPIRATION: EMPOWERING THE MIND

Inspiration is the result of the fourth, or Faith power of mind. Inspiration enables one to see what ought to be done in every situation. It gives one wisdom to know how everything is most effectively done. It provides a quick skill in accomplishment. John's Revelation speaks of the eagle, which is always a symbol of inspiration, having both wisdom and beauty.

Inspiration occurs when you've steadily ignored the appearances of difficulty around you. When things looked dark and hard, you didn't allow your mind to think about them at all; you thought only of God, the Spirit. You ignored the appearance and kept hold of the highest Principle you had. Then, there came a blankness: you felt devoid of ideas, of power.

This is the moment of inspiration, the blankness of a clear paper, upon which you may write what you like. Declare in this moment that, as the One Mind, you do not believe in foolishness or ignorance; no treatment equals the denial of accusations of foolishness or ignorance for bringing forth inspiration. Declare that, as Spirit, your judgment is perfect judgment. Declare the Truth of your being, "I know all things; I can do all things." Nothing can stand before that one idea that comes up out of the void of creation, and you will see and do the work of the Christ Spirit, in wisdom and in strength.

The Buddha said, "A fool does not know when he commits evil deeds." Since there is no evil, there can be no fool. Wisdom is the only Truth. The wise therefore know all actions as spiritual; drink all water as cups of strength, breathe all air as the energy of omnipotence, and so know no failure, no decay. The wise know no evil and no sickness: they know neither exists.

The strong one says, "I can!" The wise one says, "I know!" The one who knows perfect judgment says, "I know what to do and I am able to do it, therefore I will do it."

Right now, you are wise and immortal, free, strong, and at peace. Can you expect to feel your own true nature and delight in your estate, if you keep talking of your limitations and lacks? Near at hand is the Heavenly City. While we have called it distant — in time or space — how could we expect it to be near? Right here, visible to us, is the Heavenly Land. Could we expect it to show us its beauties if we talked of its being invisible?

Come O people! Let us all together cross the upper bar of judgment, laying hold of the Hands that, stretching toward us, draw us into fearless wholeness! Let us all together be born into the Above! Let us not look back to Chaldea or Egypt or India for the great secret of miracle-working life! Let us look to the Upper Country close at hand! For "homeward is the Tao's course."

GUIDELINES FOR TREATMENT

If a case comes before you a fifth time, it's because you haven't touched that person's judgment. You haven't struck the chord of their will. Why not? Because your own judgment has a veil before it. What veil? The veil is your persistent habit of detecting ignorance and stupidity in people, and wailing about your own foolishness or ignorance. Each time you've seen that you didn't know something, you've called yourself ignorant. Each time you've felt you made a poor choice you've called yourself foolish. And if you saw that someone else didn't seem to know something you thought they ought to, it was on your tongue, or in your mind, that they were either foolish or ignorant. This is the fall of humanity. This is all the fall there is: yielding to appearances.

Spirit is truthful and takes us at our word. Spirit supposes nothing; it believes all things. Spirit brings all its power to the words, "I am," and "I will." "Pray as if ye had received," said Jesus. The Muslim Caliph, Ali, called us to rest from seeking our good and recognize that it is seeking us.

If we detract from the merits of others, picking flaws in them, we get weaker and weaker. Accusations and criticisms are prejudices against people, and they keep the Good Mind from speaking through us. We cannot crush the tendency toward criticism; it will not be crushed. We can only deny it and so erase it from our mind. We must learn not to see ignorance or foolishness or flaws in others.

In Truth, you have the power of discernment so strong that any source—any child, book, man, woman, or broadcasting station—can tell you anything you ask, instantly. Judging that they cannot, or judging that you yourself cannot, is the only veil before your mind, the only block to the experience of instantaneous information. And you can tell when that veil is thickest, because your problem comes up again and again, and your patients come back a fifth time or appear weak and discouraged.

Don't let another person's discouragement pervert your judgment. Touch the chord of their will. Isn't that will to be free, wise and strong? If you mentally unload that person of all the yielding to appearances they've ever done, they will spring up and respond to that touch of your judgment. If your patient has talked hard on the dark and feeble side, or complains and whines in a discouraged manner, it's the very best sign that their belief in sickness is on its very last legs. And, if a patient or troubling situation comes up a fifth time, let the powerful judgment of the Christ Self say, "I do not accuse the world or myself of foolishness or ignorance; therefore, I see clearly the prosperity and happiness of my new life, now!" Come boldly forth; the powers of omnipotence are on your side.

Hope needs faith. If you cannot believe that all you encounter are cured, then take a night or day repeating the statement of what you believe in Truth. Covenant with the Spirit to expose all as health around you. Faith is the knowledge that whatever we see with the inner eye comes to the outer eye. It is the thing as God sees it.

- Ω -

THE PRACTICE.

Friday Afternoons:

We will take Fridays to stop throwing any estimates out over others. Take every Friday afternoon to insist upon the judgment within you as knowing humanity to be the expression of the wisdom of God and therefore intelligent and wise at all times, and if you positively take the premise that you do not accuse the world, or yourself, of foolishness or ignorance, no one will ever come to you the fifth time uncured, nor will your affairs ever seem to wilt or hang heavy. Consider the following words until they are a part of your own habitual thought—then let Spirit speak for you its Truth:

> I have never, as the judgment of Spirit, accused the world, or myself, of being foolish or ignorant.

With a Returning Client:

Speak the case returning a fifth time by name:

> You inherit the wisdom of the Father-Mother God; your circumstances cannot be the result of inheriting foolishness or ignorance.
>
> You are not surrounded by foolishness or ignorance; you are surrounded by the wisdom of God.
>
> Your daily associations do not burden you by the weight of foolishness, nor darken you with the darkness of ignorance; all is wisdom, from which you draw the light of wisdom every moment.
>
> You do not weigh down your own mind by willful persistence in thinking evil; you know no weakness or failure in any part of your being; you are the spiritual light that cannot fail.

> I do not persist in thinking of you as faltering or weak in any part of your being; I see you as strength, freedom, and light.
>
> Your strength is God and cannot be threatened with weakness, nor yield to weakness, in any part of your being.
>
> Your life is God and cannot be threatened with death, nor fear death, in any part.
>
> Your health is of the Spirit and cannot be threatened with, nor yield to, disease or sickness in any part of your being.
>
> You are ready to acknowledge to all around you, to yourself, and to me, that you are every whit whole, well, and happy, Now.
>
> In the name of the Father/Mother Almighty, the Miracle-working Heir, and the Mystical Holy Breath of Spirit Present, I pronounce you healed, now and forever, for it is truly so. Amen.

[These words are suggestions, only; feel free to use whatever similar words are inspired within you.]

Repeat this treatment again, before you sleep, and if any other words come to you as you are treating this case, be sure to use them.

Periodically:

Train your mind to hold a position: take your life in your hand for six days, speaking of your own spiritual nature as it was at the time of your birth in this flesh. Take each year of your life and deny that there are any causes, or results of causes, in you or around you, that could lead to any experience of disease, poverty, or failure.

THE METAPHORS.

The Number: ELEVEN.

Eleven is the number of power, courage, successful adventure—the capacity to move forward. In the eleventh year, the house of the Lord was finished and Solomon said that whoever should look at the house should be set at liberty. "The eleven stars did obeisance to Joseph," meaning that every estimate falls down into nothingness before Spirit.

The Stone: Jacinth or Red Rubellite.

The perfect jacinth is the ruby. The deep red ruby is the beauty stone. "Adam" means ruddy, red with robust health and strength. The Adam form has judgment that is warming, kindling, reviving, like the wine-red fires of the ruby. When that aspect speaks it helps you. "Drink," said Jesus as he blessed the wine, "this is the blood of the new and everlasting covenant." Beauty and judgment are one in balance leading to success. Jacinth or ruby is the second stone in the Hebrew high priest's breastplate, denoting the tribe of Gad.

The Apostle: James, Son of Zebedee, Judgment.

James, the son of Zebedee and brother of John, was also called Yaacob in Hebrew (we say "Jacob"), which means "supplanter," and became known as Iamas, which means healer in Greek. This James became the leader of the Jerusalem church after Jesus ascended, and some believe that he was destined to fill the role of spiritual messiah, with Jesus as military messiah, after John the Baptist was killed.

The James faculty is located in the lower part of the solar plexus.

The beatitude for this James is, "Ye are the salt of the earth; but if the salt have lost its savor, wherewith shall it be salted? Thenceforth it is good for nothing but to be cast out..." Salt is precious throughout the East, and exchanging it is a sacred token of friendship. The salt that Elisha used to sweeten the brackish waters of the old school of theology (Lesson 2) makes beauty everywhere: the keys of heaven and earth are given to perfect judgment.

Lesson Twelve: Love—The Crown of Glory

Whoever has Love has Life, and radiates Life wherever they walk. This is the power of the twelve lessons of Jesus and of Moses and the twelve stones of the new temple. Nothing like it has ever been discovered, in power, in effectiveness, or in speed of operation.

The Apostle Paul wrote the twelfth lesson of the metaphysical Science when he said, "Love is the fulfilling of the law." Jesus, who said, "I come not to challenge the law but to fulfill it," was so filled to overflowing with love that the conditions of this world didn't concern him in the least.

His life was his doctrine, and he laid it down for his friends and disciples. Seeing their heavy miseries, he descended into miseries that seemed even greater to show them how to ascend out of them—as a fireman goes into a burning building, or a doctor into a plague-filled hospital, to save those who are experiencing distress. And, as with the fireman or doctor, Jesus' love and skill overcame those miseries, and he was never hurt by them. Loving God, Jesus loved all, and so saved the whole world.

Love is stronger than death. Pure love for a child will save the life of that child; so, as God is all, if we love God the life of all can be saved. Those who have Love have freedom from every ill, and those who have an abundance of Love, with which God fills the whole universe, can save their friends from every ill.

Jesus loved God and taught us to do the same. When his Christ Self was manifest in body, just to look at him would cure any distress. Since that Christ Self has never gone away from our side, we can look upon that Self now, and be cured of whatever ailment we've cried about.

Whoever gets into a state of overflowing, unquenchable love is manifesting the Christ Self. In that state we see no evil in anybody or anything, seeing only their Good; we receive no injury at anybody's hands; we rejoice in all that occurs. Love diffuses all with its power. Having Love, we have strength, so we radiate strength. Everything has a light and a life and a joy and a renewal of pleasure in it for us, which nothing that happens to us can destroy.

In this state, there is nothing for us to do. We are given rest, and the works of our Spirit go forth into the world. This is the highest state of ministry possible — without thinking or trying in any way to help our neighbors we are yet their health and their joy.

This is the power of the twelfth lesson. At the sound of this lesson, the rains of charity and mercy will fall on the great deserts of your life and they will bloom with happiness: the Sahara will spring up with roses, corn, and grapes.

SIGNS & SYMBOLS

We can tell whether we've been filled with the over-flowingly grateful love of this twelfth lesson by the things and people we see. As an accusation will bring a person to us who complains of illness, a sincerely felt thankful and praise-full word brings a happy and healed case to our sight.

A deaf or blind person in your life is a sign of some willfulness on your part. It's a sign that you would not see a plain truth or hear a truth that somebody told you at some time—you persisted in seeing your own way.

The curves and lines of the face display what we focus on. So, because the good judgment of the eleventh lesson marks a face with beauty, a homely face is a sure sign that you've been accusing people of being foolish and ignorant. If you yourself are homely, it's yourself you've been accusing. If you see large crowds of plain-looking people, it signifies that you've been making such accusations all your life.

If you see many infirm and wizened people, you've been accusing certain individuals that they know little or nothing. Ingratitude is a painter of hard lines on a face, but as we have a grateful feeling towards everything and everybody, the curves and smiles will change. Did you ever see a calm, benign countenance? It shows that you once said calm, peaceful words, and thought that way, in harmony with your words. A young woman held an image of Jesus the Nazarene close to her heart and loved it so much that her face began to resemble it remarkably.

Money, or gold, is a symbol of the rich bounty of the Creator-Sustainer; the topaz is a sign of great achievement; the amethyst tells you everything is good and wise and satisfied.

But do not lay too much stress upon any kind of sign or symbol; none of these is the thing itself. When you look at any object, speak its meaning: that is its life and substance. If that substance doesn't increase soon for you, then you have been ungrateful or cynical and its nature is buried away from you.

PRAISE AND GRATITUDE UNDO COMPLAINTS

There is only one "don't" in the Science of metaphysics: DON'T COMPLAIN. Whatever we do, we are not to grieve, lament, wail, or mourn. Nothing limits our Understanding, or the Power flowing through you, like grief. The prophet Nehemiah, in 445 B.C.E., told the people not to grieve or mourn at all; he understood that whining or complaining or grieving reduces our spiritual feeling. You cannot cry (that is, be overwhelmed with sadness) and heal at the same time.

Some people think they would be satisfied if they only had this, or accomplished only that. Not so! If they mourn now, they'd find something to mourn about then. Simply give thanks for the Good in everything, now. Give great thanks.

If you look at the events of your life as making you sad and hard, you must cancel that thought and see the good they have done you in a way that makes you thankful. It may seem that your childhood was filled with pain or distress, which makes it difficult to be praise-full as an adult. One teacher used to talk to herself at each age of her life. First, as a newly born perfect child of the Spirit, then, as she was one year old, then two, and so forth, she told the little thing she had been what a miracle of God would be wrought for her someday. Then when she came to the current year, she would pronounce the whole miracle already completed. She would fill all her years with the sensation of the Spirit's loving presence, protection, and fulfillment. Then she would give thanks.

If anybody speaks to you critically, listen carefully. There is a piece of news for you about your own tendency to criticize and condemn—yourself or others—

and you will take that tendency and deny it, which will create a space for new praises for Wisdom and gratitude to the divine Self of you for speaking to you and guiding you into your higher Good.

Cynicism is a form of ingratitude that brings the most extraordinary people around us and hides the true nature of things. But now your denials of accusing others are breaking down your stubbornness. You begin to listen meekly, gladly, willingly to every voice, recognizing the Truth being spoken in it. As you continue to hold your Principle, you'll be quick to detect the true and the false ring in what you hear, and the false will not count with you—you'll forget it.

If you feel low-spirited and dissatisfied, you need not negate or deny your circumstances—you need only describe the Good of your circumstances. You have simply lost sight of the Good for a moment, and describing your Good will bring it into sight again. The effect of praise of True Intelligence in all is to bring beauty and good judgment into view, everywhere.

Do you recall how Jesus gave thanks, when Lazarus was buried, cold and still? He had waited to treat his friend as a demonstration of our tendency to delay our praises—and now his friend had been declared dead. So give thanks to the Spirit that it always does everything good for you, that it supplies you, pays your debts, and in every way blesses you. Then, like Jesus, speak to the situation in which the Good seems buried. Speak in a loud voice, praising its real meaning, and call it to come forth with new life, new kindness, new bounty, new understanding, a delightful disposition, and good conditions for all. Like Lazarus, it will rise and come forth at your calling.

TRANSCENDENCE

The twelfth lesson sets aside the doctrine of limitations. If someone sets their mind steadily to the premise that they are a limited being, that word "limit" will put a stop to their progress. But when you have learned this last lesson, you not only have power, you have all power. Having risen above condemnation, you are free, not from just one accusation; you are free from all accusation entirely. Having moved from shining mountain top to shining mountain top through each of these lessons, at this twelfth lesson you are like the eagle, soaring above the earth, surveying the landscape in perfect serenity and security: you see the whole ground of the law beneath your feet; you will have fulfilled the Law, which, being infinite, is beyond limitation.

The axiom of the twelfth lesson is: "Those who know Me transcend Me." Whoever truly knows the Self that I AM has transcended beyond the God he or she imagined before.

You know that those who truly love you find virtues in you beyond what you believe yourself to possess. And you know that the great virtues you see in your neighbor must be in yourself: we easily see in others what we may not appreciate in our own nature, but, as seeing them inspires our gratitude and praise, those very qualities begin to show up in our own lives to an even greater degree—so we transcend that which we know.

If you see adversity as the hand of God bestowing bounty, and give thanks for that bounty, calling for it to come plainly into your sight, you have touched all twelve lessons at once. It's not that God ever chooses adversity through which to give to you, but that you, having neglected to express your appreciation at the earliest opportunity, have covered your bounty and buried it in apparent adversity. But your bounty lies there, like a hungry seed, waiting for your praises to bring it forth.

It's our life's business to translate the Truth within into visible manifestation. We do this by first thinking the highest Truth we can, then speaking it, and then fixing it into everything around us. We must mix the idea we have in our mind with the word that most nearly expresses that idea. We must mean exactly what we say. Zoroaster said, "Taking the first step with good thought, the second step with good word, the third step with good deed, I enter Paradise." If our thoughts and words agree, we can't help but bring forth the Good in our lives.

It's our ministry to discover the Truth of those around us and bring that forth into visible manifestation. Repetition of the twelfth premise of this Science will make it easy to see the amethyst gem of Truth that is laying there in the heart of our neighbor, ready to be called forth.

The great wisdom-power within you is ready to spring up whenever you see wisdom expressed in a book, or someone else, or even if you see for a second the wisdom of the flies and spiders in your garden. Think of your acquaintances and make a list of what is beautiful in them, remembering and appreciating how their loveliness looked. Remember all the Goods in your life. In so doing, you're gathering "all the tithes in the storehouse," of your memory, and it was prophesied that whoever did this would spill over with blessings.

Recognizing Good is what makes us good enough to show goodness. It's wise to say frequently that everything we see, hear, smell, taste, feel, and think delights us, and we are utterly satisfied. You can see that if the air, skies, trees, men, women, and all creatures are filled with the Spirit of Good, we shall increase our love of God, or All-That-Is, by seeing this Good. Whenever you see health or strength or prosperity, or power of any kind, and don't whine or complain that you don't have them, the seeds of these within you are instantly fed—and the more that you see this way, the more you can see. Ultimately, when you see health, peace, prosperity, wisdom, balance, everywhere, you are in the Mind of God.

GUIDELINES FOR TREATMENT

If a case comes the sixth time to you, you may be certain that you've been complaining and whining about somebody or something, but joyous praise, overflowing from your loving heart, would bring them well and grateful to see you. The pleasant, happy mind is a health-giver. You must transform your moments of complaining by praise and descriptions of the Good in the universe.

So, should a case appear a sixth time, it's a signal to speak your praises. Tell them you rejoice that they are giving the free Spirit unrestrained freedom through their lives. Praise them for every virtue, every power every beauty you can think of. You need not negate any disease; you need not negate your past complaining. You must just praise and describe the Good in them which has hitherto been buried away from your awareness. Express your gratitude for their presence in your life. Soon happiness will bubble over and glisten from you, to the mind of the one who has come a sixth time and they will leap up for joy at their healing.

CLAIMING OUR BIRTHRIGHT

We have a marvelous birthright: all knowledge, all wisdom, all health, all substance, all beauty: All That Is. We take hold of this birthright by holding the knowledge of these twelve lessons in our minds. Understanding is formless, but it formulates. As each of us holds one of these ideas in our mind, it will work its way through our experience and through all the mind of the world, for a true idea lives on an on forever, while false ideas fall somewhere and fail.

Sometimes it may be hard to believe that we dwell in Spirit and that Spirit is manifesting in us. We may feel that the omnipotent God seems far off. At such times, giving thanks and praise to the Supreme I AM isn't enough to free us from our past complaints. So give thanks to the universe, to your ancestors, to your loved ones, your neighbors and associates, to yourself, to the animals you encounter, to everything you have dealings with each day, and to the divine Self within you. Feel and appreciate the unlimited beauty of Love operating in and through everyone and everything around you. This will bring Spirit back into your immediate circle quickly and effectively.

Sometimes it may seem that hardships meet us at every turn: we may feel filled with heavy ideas, our very breath deepening our anxieties. This is why the ancients taught that our breath is the path of the life-force. Hindu, Buddhist, and shamanic traditions around the world have advised people to breathe in the life of Good: to entirely empty the lungs of breath, and then to draw in a new breath with an affirmation of Good, praising the Life power as it moves through the lungs and into the body.[65] With this kind of conscious breathing, only healing Life moves through our bodies and affairs.

Sometimes it may seem that the thoughts or actions of those around us limit us. Yet men may gather all the gold of the world into a lump and say you can't have any, but by some way of the Spirit you will come out with more abundant riches than all the rest put together. They may hold debates and try psychological tricks to chain your mind or change it, but the Spirit will make a way for you to keep you free from all such attempts. You will elude every mental and material opposition, even as Jesus overcame the belief that he was dead.

Sometimes it may seem that new troubles, or new pains, afflict us each day, or that our bodies seem to be aging. Sometimes we may start to believe that we must take some medication or drug to ease them. These appearances can all be traced to the bondage of the mind to some idea or other. But Spirit is free. Knowing all things but independent of all things, Spirit will take you out of the clutches of your ideas — even the ones that label taking drugs or medications as "bad."

---

[65] This is the tradition of *prana yoga*, and is often practiced by chanting one's affirmations, the classics being *"nam myoho renge kyo"* or *"om, mane padme hum."*

The twelve lessons of the Science of metaphysics are all ideas: ideas with living meanings. In this Science we don't get attached to any ideas, since when we are tied to a notion that we would like to see all the world a certain way, we may as well be tied to a stake. Breathe out the old ideas and breathe in descriptions of all that you are glad about. You'll rise above the ideas of your world; free from them. You'll rise above even the idea of freedom, since it implies bondage and you are neither free nor bound, but above that plane. You are neither superior to it nor inferior, but beyond — for Spirit never gets caught on the hooks of any one idea. In Spirit, they're all good. Ideas are born of the Mind. Mind is God. God is ideas and more than ideas. So ideas are all good, but we don't drag ourselves around by any of them.

Sometimes it may seem that there's too much to know to be effective or good in this world. But Spirit doesn't need to go to school; Spirit knows all things. Spirit doesn't even need to be taught what is Good; Spirit is above human ideas of virtue, since hating something as a "vice" may lead to accusations, which are self-condemning. We do Good because we love the Good, not because we're afraid somebody might not like something, or from some idea that it will lead to some form of evil. Salvation by faith is having the faith in the Good that enables us to see Good everywhere and in everything.

Our birthright is a perfect world — Paradise. To claim it, you must begin describing the perfection of the world in which you live, now. You are glad that the free Spirit flows through the airs; tell it you are glad. You think your neighbor is a beautiful soul; tell her soul, mentally, that you are glad it's so beautiful. The skies are lovely with a spiritual loveliness; tell their loveliness how glad you are that it is visible to you. The stars resting against the darkness are wonderful with a spiritual wonder; tell them how glad you are to experience that wonder. The deep night is stately peace. The empty sands of the wilderness is the easiest place in the world to find the companionship of Spirit. The bustle of the streetcar or subway is an opportunity to hear what Spirit is saying. Praise it all.

The power of the Spirit is in the heart, and the wellspring of our life is fed by the meanings of our words. It's the meanings of our words that go over the world like angels of mercy, changing all the thoughts of humankind. Some people don't quite feel the meanings of the words they use, but their use of the words will, by and by, break out the meanings in their mind.

As you absorb the meaning of this twelfth lesson, you need not talk of overcoming; there is nothing to overcome. The Spirit is one with your understanding. It's one with you.

Nothing is left for us to wish for when the twelve lessons of this Science have poured out their twelve results upon our life. For with the last polish of these lessons on your character, you see that there is nothing whatever to do. You need not even talk of freedom, for there is nothing to be freed from. All is Spirit. All was, and is, and ever will be, the finished work of Divine Mind.

- Ω -

THE PRACTICE

Saturday Afternoons:

Take Saturday afternoons for praising your world. Create an opportunity to experience the wonder of this world, saying that you are satisfied with it, describing it as the perfect manifestation of Divine Mind.

> I am satisfied with the world in which I walk. All things please me. The Good is near at hand and far off. All that I see, all that I encounter are the creations of the living Good: perfect, harmonious, and satisfying.

This is a good idea on which to work out your happiness. Having your mind filled with this idea, you can't have any other idea in it.

With a Returning client:

Speak the name of a client or situation that has come forward a sixth time. Hold them in your mind as you let Spirit speak through you along the following lines:

> You are a perfect manifestation of the living God: spiritual, luminous, fearless, free. You reflect all the universe of Good.
>
> From every direction, everywhere, come words of Truth, making you know that you are free, wise, and happy.
>
> You are satisfied with the world in which you live.
>
> You show forth to the world, health, wisdom, peace.
>
> You show to me perfect health in every part of your being.
>
> You are fearless, free, strong, wise, and able to do everything that is yours to do each day. God works through you to will and to do that which is most fulfilling for you, each day.

> You are a living demonstration of the power of Truth to set free into health and strength for living service to the world.
>
> You acknowledge to the world that you are every whit whole.
>
> You acknowledge to yourself and to me that you are well and strong and alive, through and through.
>
> God, the Creator-Sustainer of the universe, is your life, health, strength, and support, forever and ever.
>
> In the name of the Father/Mother Almighty, the Miracle-working Heir, and the Mystical Holy Breath of Spirit Present, I pronounce you well and strong.
>
> As God saw the works of creation to be Good, so I see you Good. All is Good, forever and ever. Amen.

[These words are suggestions, only; feel free to use whatever similar words are inspired within you.]

Sunday:

The Sunday affirmation of this Science is:

> While knowing all things and doing all things, I am independent of all things. I am absolutely free!

Take part of each Sunday, each "Lord's Day," alone, and write or speak to some heretofore unreachable person in your world — you need not send the letter or share the words with anyone, for the thoughts of your heart must touch them. Remind them of the Truth of their being, joining the company of angels who see only the good in each of us.

THE METAPHORS

The Number: TWELVE

Twelve is the ultimate empowerment, through Revelation of Truth from the heart. "The twelfth lot came forth to Jakim." Jakim, the true high priest with King David, is not human-taught, but taught from above. It is the rest in which our works go forth, the highest state of ministry possible. The author of the Book of Revelation has a vision that speaks to the seven churches and opens the seven seals, only to discover the glory of the twelve diadems.

The Stone: Amethyst

The amethyst is the symbol of the miracle-working power of love. It's the stone of rest and empowerment, freedom and true security; the stone of the resurrection, the ascension, the New Kingdom, where love fills the human mind and overflows to the world, awakening the same love to shine back. It is that love that is stronger than death, stronger than poverty, stronger than swords, stronger even than crucifixion and the tomb. The amethyst stone has all the hues of all the stones; look into it and you will see all the other stones shining there: the blue of the sapphire, the red of the ruby, the gold of the topaz, the white of the diamond — with only the occasional touch of green, for green stands mostly for works. While it may be the least precious of the twelve gems, it is the greatest in meaning. It covers the twelfth wall of the New Jerusalem and is the first stone in the Hebrew priest's breastplate, standing for the tribe of Asher, or "revelation."

The Apostle: Simon Peter

Simon Peter is the English version of the Greek, Simon Petros. His Hebrew name would have been Shimon, or Shimehon, meaning "listener," with the nickname Cephos, which is a common reference in Aramaic to being "dense as a stone." Simon, the big fisherman who cared for his wife and mother-in-law with great gentleness, was somewhat slow at grasping spiritual concepts, but once he got them, he didn't let go — instead proclaiming them with his very being for the rest of his life.

In the gospel stories, Jesus calls big old Simon, "Peter, the rock upon which I will build my church," because of his recognition of and faith in Jesus' messiahship. Yet the stories tell us that Peter blundered on several occasions, most famously by drawing his sword when Jesus was being arrested and, while Jesus was being held on trial, by fearfully denying ever having known him — three times "before the cock crowed." As often happens, those blunders became the basis for Peter's amazingly powerful work as an apostolic missionary — especially to Rome. He became the first bishop of Rome, called il Papa, the Pope, and all Popes since are said to walk "in the shoes of the fisherman," Simon Peter.

Simon Peter is associated with the heart chakra, as one who listens, and speaks, from the heart.

The Beatitude for Peter is "Ye are the light of the world..." as it is through our apparent blunders that our light becomes visible. As apparent curses are turned into blessings, we have experienced the divine alchemy — the irritating grain of sand in the oyster becomes the lustrous pearl.

Part Two: Commentaries

Emma Curtis Hopkins' work fits into a specific time and place: the United States of America at the turn of the nineteenth into the twentieth century. Electricity was just becoming available. Automobiles and the telephone, also. Einstein's theory of Relativity had not yet been published, and women did not yet have the vote. Clearly, much of what she said, and how she said it, can be understood in terms of the time and place in which she lived.

At the same time, her work is timeless. Drawing as she did on the wisdom of many ages and many cultures, seeking always to find the Truth behind the common understanding, Emma transcended her time. As a result, modern scientific research supports and expands on the concepts that she presented over a hundred years ago.

The Historical Context

The body of material laid out in this text is based on the ideas of a very unusual woman who grew up on a farm in mid-nineteenth century New England, then lived into the 1920s, making several trips across North America and Europe. Through her reading, her practice and her teaching, she was able to transcend the limitations that were placed on her by her culture.

But these ideas were not entirely hers. They were based on her study of many people's work, including most notably, Mary Baker Eddy, the founder of Christian Science, and that remarkable woman's teacher, the inventor Phineas Parkhurst Quimby of Maine. Both of these had established beyond doubt that it was possible for chronically and critically injured or diseased people to regain full health with no other treatment than words spoken and thought. Between them thousands of people were treated and hundreds of cases were documented as cured, of people who had experienced great pain or other distressing symptoms, often having been treated without success by physicians.

In her search for "a line of reasoning," however, Emma went beyond Quimby and Eddy to the teachings of Ralph Waldo Emerson, Margaret Fuller, and Bronson Alcott, leaders of the Transcendentalist movement in her native New England, and to their teachers, Imanuel Swedenborg, the great Swedish mystic, and Johann von Goethe, Germany's great metaphysician. She drew support not only from Biblical texts, as she'd been taught by Mrs. Eddy, but from the great spiritual writings that were then beginning to come in translation from India, Persia, China, and Egypt, as well. She read everything that came her way, from the Bible to the *Bhagavad Gita*, Voltaire to Tolstoy, Plato to Cicero — often in the language in which it was originally written.

DISCOVERED TEXTS

Much of what Emma taught about the Bible would have been considered heretical during her lifetime. However, discoveries and scholarship over the past fifty years, and recent translations from the Aramaic of many of the Gospel statements, have tended to support her ideas. The Dead Sea Scrolls have helped us to understand that there was much more to Jesus' teachings than had been understood before, and archaeological evidence shows that many "pious legends" have no foundation in historical record, while other stories, assumed by many scholars to be invented, have been substantiated.[66]

Now, with the uncovering of the Gnostic codices near the ancient Nag Hammadi monastery in Egypt, our generation knows that there's much more to the mystical teachings of Jesus than heretofore understood, and we have access to a deeper understanding of the Christ concept than traditional teachings have allowed.

The Christian Gnostic movement was based on the idea that we need to go inside to discover Truth, and that the Christ mind is at the center of our being. This understanding of Christianity was contrary to much of

---

[66] For example, in India stories tell of a teacher, known as "St. Issa," who came from the Mediterranean, studied in many Hindu and Buddhist communities, mastered the highest *yogas*, then returned to his homeland where he was killed by the Empire for his teachings.

what was said in the Pastoral Epistles attributed to Paul, and was almost completely wiped out as heresy when the Roman Church became the religion of the Roman Empire under Constantine and his successors, but is very much in alignment with Emma's teaching. The Gospel of Thomas gives a good example.

> Jesus said: "If they say to you, "Whence have you come?" say to them, "We came from the light, the place where the light came into existence through itself alone."...If they say to you, "[who are] you?" say, "We are his sons and we are the elect of the living Father.' If they ask you, "What is the sign of your Father who is within you?" say to them, "It is a movement and a rest" (# 51; scroll 89-90).[67]

A third branch of inquiry that supports Emma's interpretation is the work of George Lamsa, Rocco Erico, and Janet Magiera, who have found and translated ancient scrolls that were written in Aramaic, the language Jesus spoke, rather than Greek, the language of Paul's churches. Many of Emma's ideas are borne out when we see the interpretation of Jesus' idioms from the perspective of his listeners.

Of these, perhaps the most significant is her translation of the "seven last words" attributed to Jesus on the cross: "*Eli, Eli, Imana sabachthani!*" This sentence literally means, "Master, Master, for this was I separated!" and the idiom means "this was my destiny," or "I was born for this." The notion that Jesus was quoting Daniel's cry in the wilderness (usually translated as "My God, My God! Why have you forsaken me!") is invalidated by the fact that a man of his time would have recited sacred scripture in the Hebrew in which

---

[67] From Robert Grant & David Freedman, *The Secret Sayings of Jesus*, 1960.

he'd learned it, rather than translating it into the colloquial Aramaic.

Cultural studies of the time provide further insight into the nature of New Testament teachings. Philosophers have found significant parallels between the Gospel teachings and those of popular Greek philosophers of the period. Hebrew scholars have long pointed out that Rabbi Hillel taught many of the "heretical" ideas that are ascribed to Jesus during the same years. And historians have found that many men were seen as the hoped-for "Messiah" by distraught Israelites seeking a savior from the burdens of Rome in those days—some of whom also were wandering healers. Further, observers in other countries over the centuries have described a variety of "miraculous" healings, supporting Emma's understanding that, while Jesus the Nazarene was the most complete example of someone who embodied the principles of applied metaphysics, all humanity has the potential to become healers through the power of word and thought.

MODERN SCIENCE

Though written in the language of religion, Emma worked from a model of human experience that has been borne out across the sciences. She herself was an avid student of mathematics, chemistry, and the then emerging studies of electricity.

It's not too surprising, therefore, that Emma's view of the universe is far more consistent with that of modern quantum physics than with the classical Newtonian clockwork that was the prevalent theory of her time. She presents matter as made up of "Substance" that is neither matter nor energy and yet everywhere at all times—much like the "quantum field" or subatomic "wavicles" or "strings" described by quantum physicists, today. She also says that our thoughts affect this Substance that underlies all matter—as has been proven over and over again as observers have affected experimental results in the linear accelerators and cyclotrons of quantum physics. She further says that such action is immediate, regardless of distance or apparent intensity, which may be described in terms of the physical concept of "entanglement" or the instantaneous "nonlocal" effect of action on one "wavicle" that has been in contact with another.

Emma's principle that thoughts shape our bodies and affect our immune system is one that scientists in the field of psychoneuroimmunology have been establishing more and more clearly in recent decades. Francisco Varela and Humberto Maturana coined the term "autopoesis" to describe this process, and Carl Simonton developed a remarkably effective process for reducing or eliminating cancer cells based on the patient's visualization of the cells' destruction and disappearance.

Thousands of anecdotes and hundreds of well-designed studies have established the positive effect of prayer, whether or not the patient or the one praying believes in prayer or in God, supporting Emma's assertion that our clear and powerful sense of the Good as here and now must enhance the wellbeing of those around us. Also supportive are the many studies establishing a relationship between healthiness and the acceptance of a higher power working in one's life.

Emma posits that all matter, conditions, and circumstances are temporary structures, maintained only by the energy of our thoughts and attention. This understanding corresponds to the principles developed by Nobel laureate Ilya Prigogine, who defined such systems as "dissipative structures."

Her description of faith and other mental states as having a tendency to increase once started is a perfect example of what is called, in cybernetics, a "positive, reinforcing loop," and reinforcing or counteracting such loops is the aim of most modern behavioral psychologists. It's also the essence of the work of Byron Katie, and the workshops and books offered by Joe Dispenza.

Finally, her concept of a single intelligence pervading all the universe is totally consistent with emerging theories of panpsychism, in which the underlying quantum field is recognized as consciousness, everywhere present.

So the principles she taught as spiritual Truths are being borne out in modern science as physical realities. As the research continues, and more and more connections are made between mind and body, we can look forward to more experimental evidence supporting the concepts put forth in Emma Hopkins' books and lectures.

The Principles in the Language of Science

To paraphrase Emma's principles in modern scientific language, we could state the essence of each of her lessons as something like the following:
1. The universe is one interwoven holon,[68] the material and energetic manifestation of an underlying intelligence that is evident in the patterns of order and harmony present at all levels; all patterns within the whole emerge out of the underlying creative intelligence; all beings are a part of that whole, and intelligence and harmony are part of our essential nature.
2. In the one whole that is the universe, there can be no separation; all the "wavicles" or "strings" that make up matter and energy are interconnected such that any action in any part of the universe acts on all of it, nonlocally, throughout space and time; I am therefore one with all things everywhere, and with all that makes up all things, so my only sustainable experience is the harmony of the interconnected whole; any other experience is a dissipative structure[69] that depends on continuous flows of thought or attention for its existence and can be dissolved

---

[68] the Greek term describing an indivisible whole, within which anything affecting a part, affects all.
[69] Ilya Prigogine's Nobel-Prize winning concept that says that most structures of the universe are maintained by a flow of energy/information into and through them, and that a change in the inflow may cause the structure to dissipate/dissolve or, in certain circumstances, reform into a new structure.

easily by re-focusing energy and creative intelligence on the whole or other aspects of the whole.
3. As I am one with all things everywhere and across all time, I have access to all knowledge of all beings, all emotional states, and all possible activities; my life is a pattern within the totality of these states and activities; it emerges from the particular aspect of the creative intelligence that is my imagination, and whatever I imagine becomes my experience — either effortlessly sustainable, or a dissipative structure that requires continued energy for its continued existence.
4. Since I have access to all possibilities at all times, my experience is a function of what I have chosen to accept; to the extent that I choose to experience only those patterns of possibility that reflect and reinforce the harmonious whole of which I am a part, I effortlessly and enjoyably experience those; therefore I choose to hold those patterns firmly in my mind and imagination, regardless of all appearances.
5. Because all patterns of matter and energy in the universe emerge out of creative intelligence, all of my experience emerges from my particular aspect of creative intelligence, or imagination; there is no other source of experience and to the extent that I align my imagination, thoughts, and words with the pattern of the whole, I experience harmony and the oneness of the whole.
6. The intelligence that manifests as my particular pattern of matter and energy in this holon we call the universe is capable of understanding the

underlying pattern of the whole and expressing it in ways that enable me to re-align any patterns across space and time; I need simply to focus my attention on the underlying and overarching pattern of harmony that lays beyond the realm of my present experience.
7. thru 12. I can apply these principles with and for all other beings whom I encounter, just as I can for my own experience — negating that which is not an aspect of the whole, affirming that which is, holding fast to my choice, and ultimately experiencing and expressing only the harmony of the interconnected whole, which we call Unconditional Love.

Emma was a product of her time and her culture, but her wisdom and power to affect others' lives transcends both. May you find her principles and practices as effective and useful as did the many thousands of people who studied with her and became healers and teachers in their own right, over a hundred years ago.
–rlm

PART THREE

Emma Hopkins' The Radiant I AM[70]

The listening disciple becomes a preaching apostle. Standing at the Center of Being and looking outward over the world, instruction is received from every quarter. But who hath told himself that all the objects he beholds and all their movements also are but projections of his own judgment? He seems always to be a learner and a seeker till at the center of his consciousness the fact is suddenly proclaimed that he himself produced the world as it appears.

Then he no longer listens to informations from without; he authorized from himself what he would see and hear and touch; even what he would know.

I have been a listening disciple. I have let people and objects and activities come toward me and impinge upon me till I have been over-piled and mountain-covered with thoughts. But now I know that I AM, at my own Center, authority over and through my universe, and I shall ordain my twelve disciples, or my twelve powers, to spread my Original Nature abroad till from me to the utmost stretches all is my Divine Ego.

It is the teaching that all is Spirit, and matter is but obedient shadow-picturing thereof, which is the final subtle message toward me that makes me see that I AM what I AM and alter not. Spirit is the gentle Mother doctrine among the doctrines of the world — gentle but inexorable. She brings to exposure the Christ Child, my I AM — who shall rule all nations with a rod of iron. The

---

[70] This is copied from Emma's journals, and appears to be her practice of Lesson 5, applying the power of words.

iron that is strongest is magnetic. It rules in the earth by holding all the particles together. It rules in the sun. It rules in all the spheres. They roll because of the magnet. So all my being has moved because of my I AM. So all my universe shall wheel to my ordination.

This is my ministry. I am glad to give myself to my Self and to give all my world to my Self and let my Self do in judgment twelve works upon the earth.

This is my ministry. I have heard all I shall ever hear. I know all I shall ever know. I now make my Self known.

I make my Self known by speaking, thinking, writing and living the word of my Self — my I AM. I reign from sea to sea and from the river to the uttermost parts of the earth. I reign by my knowledge of my own I AM and its last name. The name of my I AM in the last days of the manifestation of a universe, which I made by not speaking from my Central Point, is Jesus Christ. The I AM in me is Jesus Christ. I speak boldly of my Self to the world in which I walk. I think from my Self forward over its surface through all its substance. I write what I know and I write what I AM, and what I write is the fiber of all things. They shall feel themselves knitting into transfigured embodiments by my written words. "Write what thou hearest and give it unto the churches."

I live as a breath of life forward and back through the universe. I AM the conduct of my world. What I do it does. Conducting from my Center, I satisfy my world with what I AM. My world can find no flaw in Me. I can find no flaw in my Self. Because I live at my Center, ye live also. My rod of iron is my being what I AM and knowing it.

"We give Thee thanks, O Lord God Almighty, because Thou has taken to Thyself Thy great power and hast reigned!" These that are thankful are my powers. I AM Lord God Almighty to my own powers.

I AM power of Life to the universe. Because I live, all that hath form or name shall live. There shall be no death nor fear of death throughout the boundaries of eternal spaces from this day forth forever. That which proceedeth forth from Me is Life and the power of Life forever. As I breathe, the creatures of the sea and air and sands rise up refreshed and there is no power against their life and no ending of their life forever from this day forth.

I AM the unending, irresistible Life of the world. I think this—I speak this—I write this—I live this. This is my ministry which I AM. "Let us give ourselves to the ministry of the Word."

I AM the power of Health to the universe. Because I AM holy at my Center, I make whole wherever I decree. I AM authority. There shall be happy, joyous, free, fearless Health through this universe from this day. All that have name and shape shall this day lift up their heads with new refreshment. The elixirs of a fadeless healing shall steal through them. There shall be no disease or sickness from this day of the Lord onward. "The inhabitants shall not say, 'I am sick,' anymore."

I AM the unending, irresistible, beautiful Health of the whole universe, I, its Center, shed my Health abroad. This is my stopless ministry. I think this—I speak this—I write this—I live this.

I AM the power of Strength to the universe. Because I AM unalterable, I AM Omnipotence. I minister to myself abroad. All that have shape or name feel stealing through them a reviving Strength from this day which nothing shall ever interfere with. I strengthen wherever I decree. I AM Authority. There shall be lifting up and strong godliness throughout all mysteries of height and depth and plain and valley from this day onward. There shall no faintness seize upon anything. There shall no weakness touch anything. There shall no feebleness be heard of forever and forever. The prophecy is fulfilled in me which reads: "When men are cast down, thou shalt say, there is lifting up."

I Am the Strength of the universe. This is my ministry. Strength that proceedeth from me is irresistible, unending. I think this—I speak this—I write this—I live this. I AM a tower whose radiance is elixir for infinity.

I AM the power of Support to the universe. Everything that hath shape or name is upborne and prospered in all its ways from this day on. There shall be no lack or disappointed effort. All shall rise and have self-respect from this day on. I, from my Center, AM a radiance of upbearing sustainment through all this universe. There shall be no poverty, no lack, no want from this day forth.

I AM the sufficiency of my universe. It is my decree. The elixir of bounty, of prospering effort, spreads forth from me. This is my irresistible unending ministry. I think this—I speak this—I write this—I live this.

I AM a tower whose radiance sheds abroad Protection for infinite kingdoms. That which speeds forth as my radiance is the Holy Spirit of Revelation. I AM the unending peaceable defense of the whole universe. By Me all that have name or shape are safe and secure running, or walking, or flying forever. They shall not fear. They shall not be attacked. They shall not be hurt. The days of hurting have flown away. The dreams of danger are past. Things wake as my mighty elixirs spread through them borne on the streams of my word, my thought, my writings, my life breaths, They rouse themselves. They are safe forevermore. "They shall not hurt or kill in all my holy mountain."

I AM the security of the infinite stretches and of the near creations. "Peace, peace to them that are afar off and to them that are near." This is my ministry. I think this—I speak this—I write this—I live this.

I AM the power of mind to my universe. Even the stones shed a message intelligible to all other shapes and names because of my being the intelligence of all things shedding my nature forth without stopping. No foolishness or ignorance shall ever shame anything visible or invisible from this day on forever. Its Presence is its wisdom. Its Presence is its information. An elixir of intelligence is on its stopless march from me at my Center forever through all the reaches of space and formulation. I decree Intelligence. I decree Mind. I think and all the universe thinks divinely like Me. My Mind is not as the former mind which could change or stop. It is the Jesus Christ Mind whose word shall not pass away.

I AM a tower whose radiance is unending Wisdom through all things. This is my ministry. My logos. I think this—I speak this—I write this—I live this. I AM the radiant Logos in Mind.

I AM the power of Speech to my universe. My tongue is its tongue. What I say, it says from its smallest atom to its gigantic formulation. My Central Name is my tongue of radiance. All that speak, speak of the I AM. One tongue only shall speak. Its language no man or stone did hear nor could ever hear till I should speak from my Center. I now speak what I speak from my Jesus Christ Name. So atoms and angels speak a new heaven and a new earth into their own view, empowered by my tongue with its elixirs of fire. I speak and the universe uttereth itself.

I AM a tower whose radiance shed eloquent Speech through atoms and men. This is my ministry. I think this—I speak this—I write this—I live this.

I AM the power of Writing—Recording—Witnessing of Jesus Christ and the Name folded within the gates of that Name. What I write the world writes. I fix my hallowed glory with my fingers and all things fix themselves to go no more away from their home forever. The Written Word is the haven of man and of beast. I AM the inspiring pen of the world. I shall find my inspiration everywhere. Nothing unlike my writing lives. I AM from my Center the fixing and transfixing pen. I shall not faint or fail to fix my glory everywhere. I AM man's inspiration with his pen and I inspire all things to record me as I AM.

I AM a tower whose radiance is the inspiration to pen itself in its divinity in every shape and name through infinity. I think this—I speak this—I write this—I live this.

I AM the power of Song—joyous Song that steals in unquenchable smiling through the universe. I AM the Eternal Smile. As I shed my Self through the atoms and through the globes, they sing. I AM the joyous song, unquenchable, unhinderable forever. No other sound but singing, no other voice but joy is heard from this day forth.

I AM the inspiring Joy of my world forever. This is my ministry. I think this—I speak this—I write this—I live this. There is joy beyond ecstasy. I AM that Joy.

I AM the power of Skill for all things. From me there steals forever a quick touch of skillfulness through all fingers. No child needs to be schooled, no bird needs a teacher, no angel needs a helper. All can do their part and they can do what they will to do. There is no incompetency or need of learning from this day on forever, anywhere.

I AM a tower whose radiance is a skill-inspiring elixir, stopless—eternal. This is my ministry. I think this—I speak this—I write this—I live this.

I AM the power of Beauty and Judgment. From my poised place I AM the poise of the ages of men. I judge, and my judgment is what all things go by. They judge like me. I set the features of things into balance and this is their beauty. I balance the atoms that flow in the skin and its balance is its beauty. I set the inner parts into harmony be being the central judgment of eternal facts. I decree and there is no injustice. Nothing falls into mistake. Nothing is unjust. The scales of my judgment are the scales in the hearts of all men. They will not fail to use these scales. And thus order and beauty reign from Pole Star to Southern Cross and from right-hand to left of the worlds beyond worlds. "He shall not faint or fail till He hath established judgment in the earth!" I AM a scale whose rods are the beams of unbreakable right. My judgment is right judgment. As I judge, so it is.

All the poise that I AM I radiate through all the universe and all things feel the joy of adjustment. This is my ministry. This is my nature. I think this — I speak this — I write this — I live this.

I AM the power of Heaven to every atom and to every archangel. From my Jesus Christ center of Being I shed Heaven through the spaces. All things breathe of my radiance. I shed my Self abroad in unending beauty; Heaven breaks in the heart and on the vision from me to all things, through all things. The old heaven and earth sink away into forgotten dreams because I have found my Self, because I know my Self, because I AM my Self. I have taken up the authority I had from before the worlds were spun on the ethers of time.

I decree Heaven and Heaven it is. My Kingdom is come and it is the new land of delight that steals on the vision and reaches the senses of all things. Nothing like the dreams of earth, nothing like the motions of matter ever reaches my universe. As silently as a moonbeam lights on a mountain, so silently has Heaven stolen on the gazes of all the creations of infinity.

I Am a tower whose elixirs of radiance reveal the visions of Heaven to the senses of man. From my Jesus Christ center I AM Heaven from this day forth to all the universe. This is my stopless everlasting ministry. I do this. I AM this. My Name is a folding gate that opens and there is no sound. My Name is Jesus Christ, and in that Name I Am the Heaven of all this universe.

Its meaning is its influence. I AM its meaning, its influence, its heavenliness. I think this — I speak this — I write this — I live this. I AM what I AM. I do what I

AM by knowing my Self as Jesus Christ the Heaven-sending Center of Being, the Heaven-sending Me.

- Ω -

About the Authors

EMMA CURTIS HOPKINS

When Josephine Emma Curtis was born in New England, just before the Civil War, it was the early years of the women's suffrage movement. At that time women had no rights to property or even to earn a living, and most women were taught only enough to be able to read the Bible and count change for a purchase. Part of the women's suffrage effort was to find ways for women to be able to care for themselves if something happened to their husbands or if they didn't marry. Related to that effort was an emphasis on education and an exploration of healthcare professions that were less invasive and heavy-handed than the mainstream medical practice of the day. To that end, hydrotherapy, homeopathy, nursing, and various forms of tonics and "mind cures" were all considered possible avenues for a woman to explore.

Emma graduated from high school and became a classroom teacher. This was unusual in mid-nineteenth-century New England, where teaching was a man's job. But men were scarce after the Civil War, so Emma was among the first young women to step into that previously masculine role—and helped to establish the tradition of women as grammar-school teachers. She followed the normal pattern of her day when she married a colleague and had a son, inviting her sister to live with them as companion and helper.

Living in small, rather poor homes in New England as her husband moved from job to job trying to pay off the debts accrued while he was in college, it was hard for this family to maintain good health. This was the era of "consumption," a respiratory ailment that made it difficult to breathe, reducing the oxygen flow to various organs, and too often resulted in death. That respiratory illnesses were common is no surprise if we consider life during those years. Most people lived in towns in valleys, with no paved roads, fireplaces and wood stoves for heat, coal-fired furnaces in early factories, and cats, dogs, and other animals in and around the house—with no vacuum cleaners to remove dust and hair from the rugs and furniture that filled the Victorian era home. And the studious, curious, Emma was probably more interested in reading than cleaning.

Autumn of 1883 was the turn-around point for the Hopkins family. That summer a neighbor had introduced Emma to Mary Baker Eddy, who provided an informal lecture describing the philosophy and practice of Christian Science. Mrs. Eddy was convinced that she offered a way for women to contribute to their own financial well-being while providing a needed service in the community. Emma, well-read in the sciences of the day, was not impressed. However, when her little household was taken over by a "serious respiratory ailment" that no medical attention they could afford would help, she tried Mrs. Eddy's approach. With her neighbor's support and assistance, Emma moved through her own illness and was able to bring her family safely through to even greater health than before. Now she was impressed—this was something to learn more about.

Emma, as was typical for women of that day, had no funds of her own, and her husband's income was not only limited but drained by the payment of his debts. She offered to pay a deferred tuition, suggesting that whatever she might receive as a practitioner could be used to pay for her lessons. Mrs. Eddy agreed, but it appears that Emma worked for her as an editor for the Christian Science Journal, instead.

Though summarily dismissed from that post after a year, Emma always addressed Mrs. Eddy as her "dear teacher," calling herself "your devoted disciple" whenever she wrote to her. In spite of being frequently disparaged over subsequent years, she was able to maintain her respect and gratitude for the woman who opened the doors for her to a metaphysical universe in which understanding Truth could manifest Paradise. Indeed, it was essential to her system that she do so.

At that time, Chicago was a booming transportation center, providing rail, boat, and coach services to the East, Midwest, and Northwestern states. People from all over Europe were immigrating to the northern Great Plains and Chicago was the transfer point for all freight and passengers. The women's suffrage movement and the temperance society were very active, as were various metaphysical and spiritualist associations, scattered among the many Protestant churches, Catholic missions, and the usual boomtown bars and brothels. Several newspapers served the city and a number of publishing houses offered books and magazines to the surrounding areas.

As the editor of the *Christian Science Journal* Emma's name had become familiar to Christian Science students around the world. This provided her an opening in the Midwest: a temporary position editing a similar journal, called *Mind Cure* out of Chicago, which was the transition she needed to make a new start—this time with her family around her. They rented a smallish house in central Chicago, and later bought a large home that provided space for meetings and for clients to stay. Emma immediately put an ad in the daily paper offering her services as a healer and teacher of healing, while her friend Mary Plunkett set up a school for them to operate from, and in a very few months they were well-established.

This arrangement lasted only a couple of years. Mary Plunkett returned to New York in 1888, and Emma's husband and son returned to New England soon thereafter, leaving Emma to reorganize her life and work. She did so by creating a seminary, authorized by the state of Illinois, with a board and faculty drawn from former students and clients. She maintained the Hopkins Associations that she and Plunkett had created for graduates, and began a new publication to support the members.

The years that followed were remarkably productive. The Seminary graduated hundreds of students and Emma ordained many ministers, sending them out into the world to "teach the gospel, heal the sick, and cast out passions." It was during this period that the Brooks sisters began their healing ministry in Colorado, the Fillmores set up Silent Unity in Kansas, and numerous smaller ministries called "Church of Truth," "High Watch Fellowship," and many other names were established around the country. Emma wrote a regular bible study column in a Chicago paper as well as articles in the journal for her association. She was invited to speak all over the country, and in London her work became the basis for a metaphysical movement there.

The Great Chicago World's Fair and Exposition of 1893 was an opportunity for all the world to see what the Midwestern United States were producing. Emma chose this opportunity to present her work, not in the Religions Pavilion, where Mrs. Eddy's Church of Christ, Scientist was on display, but in the Women's Pavilion, where women's rights and opportunities were being showcased, including the settlement house work of Jane Adams, and various associations working for suffrage, fair labor, and temperance. Clearly, her focus was empowerment rather than formation of a religion.

In 1894, the Hopkins Association in New Orleans requested permission to open a Seminary there. The Associations were thriving around the country and it looked as if the torch were being picked up by this new group. Emma and her board agreed and the new Seminary was up and operating that fall. A year later, Emma dissolved the Chicago Seminary, relieved that she would no longer have to "possess" the things necessary to operate at that level. Now others could carry the light that she'd tended so carefully for the last decade.

So, in 1895, Emma sold everything and began a new life as an itinerant healer and teacher. For the next twenty-eight years, she spent some time each year living on her mother's farm, where she'd grown up and where her younger sister was based, and several weeks or months in various hotels and homes around the U.S. and Europe, addressing Hopkins Association meetings and working with individuals. She spent each winter, as well as a few summers, in New York, speaking and providing individual sessions to some of the greatest and least-known residents of that city. [71]

By 1918, New Thought was a significant religious movement in this country, and Emma was nominated President of the International New Thought Alliance, which is still a major organization of New Thought churches in this country. She continued to speak to groups and provide individual treatments for clients until a series of heart failures in 1923 rendered her, as she described in a letter to Mabel Dodge Lujan, "not so much sick as called to complete a career." After a year in recovery, she returned to New York, having reduced her practice to meetings with a few individual clients in her hotel.

Among these was a spiritual seeker who had made quite a reputation as a speaker, but who was still feeling as if he hadn't quite got a handle on the essence of the science: Ernest Holmes. In the fall of 1924, after several failed attempts on his part, Emma finally agreed to a meeting, which he thought would be an interview, but which turned into the first of her series of twelve lessons. When the series was complete, he had his clarity, and proceeded to write his own version of the teachings in his major work, *Science of Mind*.

Emma's last months were spent quietly on the farm in Connecticut, with her sister and occasional visitors. One April evening in 1925, so the story goes, Emma called for a former student to come read a few

---

[71] A series of letters between Emma and Mabel Luhan from this period have been found in Luhan's papers and are quoted extensively in Gail Harley's *Emma Curtis Hopkins, Forgotten Founder of New Thought*.

favorite passages from the Bible to her, and, while listening, she closed her eyes and passed on.

RUTH L. MILLER

Ruth L. Miller, Ph.D. is a 20th-century "Baby Boomer" who integrates new understandings of culture and consciousness in a way that "the rest of us" can understand.

Working as a futurist and organizational and community development consultant, she taught in half a dozen colleges and universities around the Pacific Northwest, based on her degrees in anthropology, environmental studies, cybernetics, and systems science.

In her second career, the Rev. Dr. Miller, D.D., serves as an ordained New Thought minister in Unity, Science of Mind, and Unitarian churches around Oregon. She is also the host of a regular radio program called Noetic Moments, on the science of consciousness, and manages several websites and a YouTube channel to provide broader access to her books, interviews, classes, and presentations.

Miller offers modern interpretations of the writings of early New Thought teachers, along with summary points and exercises, in her Library of Hidden Knowledge series (published by Atria/Simon & Schuster) and in several books published by WiseWoman press. She also brings a deeper understanding to the ongoing cultural processes and potentials in a series of books about how looking to the past can enhance our future published by Portal Center Press.

Her guidelines for a deeper, more effective spiritual life reach beyond traditional notions of religion, integrating the essence of humanity's many faith traditions.

Her website is: www.ruthlmillerphd.com

Books by Emma Curtis Hopkins

The Bible Series

The Genesis Series

The Gospel Series

The Judgment Series

First Lessons (1887)

Class Lessons of 1888

Drops of Gold

Scientific Christian Mental Practice

High Mysticism

Resumé

Studies in Esoteric Philosophy

Self-Treatments

To find more of Emma's work, including previously unpublished materials, go to:
 www.emmacurtishopkins.org
The website is maintained as a community service by Rev. Michael Terranova, co-director of the Emma Curtis Hopkins Study Center in Vancouver, Washington.

Books by Ruth L. Miller

Interpretations of Early Teachers
- *As We Think, So We Are. James Allen's Guide to Transformation*
- *Coming Into Freedom, H. Emilie Cady's Lessons in Truth for the 21st Century*
- *Identifying With The Infinite: Lillian DeWaters' Science of the Absolute for the 21st Century*
- *Natural Abundance, Ralph Waldo Emerson's Guide to Prosperity*
- *One Law: Henry Drummond Explains Nature and Love*
- *The Creative Power of Thought: Thomas Troward's Metaphysics*
- *The NEW Game of Life and How to Play It: Florence Shinn's classic for the 21st century*
- *The NEW Master Key System: Charles Haanel's classic for the 21st century*
- *The NEW Science of Getting Rich: Wallace Wattles' classic for the 21st century*
- *The Spiritual Science of Emma Curtis Hopkins*
- *Unveiling Your Hidden Power: Emma Curtis Hopkins' Metaphysics for the 21st Century*

Biographies and Histories in New Thought
- *150 Years of Healing: America's New Thought Healers & Teachers*
- *They Healed by Thought Alone: America's New Thought Healers & Teachers* (3rd edition of *150 Years of Healing*)
- *Paths of Power* series of biographies — Emerson, Holmes, The Fillmores, Cady, Hopkins, Troward

Self Help & Spiritual Support
- *Spiritual Success: Developing Your Own Daily Practice*
- *Uncommon Prayer: Beyond Religious Formulas*
- *Unlocking the Power of The Secret: 12 Keys*
- *Experiencing the Miracle: The Essential Course In Miracles for the 21st Century*

Healing Methods & Consciousness
- *Calm Healing: Mind-Body Healing Methods* with Robert B. Newman
- *Empowered Care: Mind-Body Medicine* (2nd edition of *Calm Healing*) with Robert B. Newman

Organization Development
- *Developing 3rd Generation Learning Communities: A Heuristic Discovery Process* with Kazimierz Gozdz
- *Organizations with Spirit: from Vision thru Staffing*

Our Culture's History and Future
- *Apocalypse Now? Unveiling rather than Destroying*
- *Earth Can Still Be Home: Creating Humanity's Future* (3rd edition of *Living A New Dream*)
- *Home: Creating Humanity's Future* (2nd edition of *Living A New Dream*)
- *Language of Life: finding solutions to today's issues in ancient languages* with Milt Markewitz
- *Madonna, Magdalene, and Beyond* (2nd edition of *Mary's Power: the divine feminine hidden in western culture*)
- *To Rebalance Earth: Indigenous Wisdom for A Harmonious Future* with Milt Markewitz

COMMENTS FROM READERS

"Ruth's introduction to Emma reveals a woman seeking truth who through fierce intellectual study and divine revelation created a system of thinking about our human/god experience.
    These teachings provide the framework I've been seeking for an exciting and empowered reality that transcends the illusions of the material life." –Alex

"Thank you so much for allowing me to receive all these wonderful teachings. I have made another shift in my life to bring all Good into it. This fits right in my resolving all issues. ..." Ursula

"What Emma offers us is a way of sorting through all of the concepts that we have picked up over the years from all of the books we have read and workshops and seminars we have participated in and churches we have attended and knowing which ones to discard. She then provides us with a daily practice by which we can hone our remaining belief system to the point that Truth rises to the top of our lives like cream in a bottle of whole milk and we begin to live a different sort of life — one that is truly spiritual." –Nelson

Made in the USA
Las Vegas, NV
15 April 2025